Anna Andlauer

The Rage to Live

The International D.P. Children's Center
Kloster Indersdorf 1945-46

In memory of Greta Fischer (1910-1988)

About this Book

This book was first published in German in 2011: **Zurück ins Leben. Das internationale Kinderzentrum Kloster Indersdorf 1945-46**, Antogo Verlag, Nuremberg.
http://www.antogo-verlag.de

The book you read now, **The Rage to Live. The International Children's Center Kloster Indersdorf 1945-46**, is a revised edition of the German book translated by **Tobe Levin**, an associate of Harvard University. It is also available as an eBook, published by the Author: http://www.amazon.com/dp/B008F5DRCU

Copyright © Anna Andlauer 2012
Aufhauser Str. 20, D-85258 Weichs
ISBN 978-1479322893
All rights reserved.

Printed and distributed by
CreateSpace Independent Publishing Platform.

Hebrew names and terms have been transcripted by US spelling rules. Minor inconsistencies in the citations are adjusted, additions and grammatical changes are enclosed in square brackets.

Contents

About this Book 2
Preface 5
Foreword 8
Help for Survivors 15
Helpers in the Pioneer Project 20
    Displaced Children arrive 25
    Jewish child survivors 27
    Gentile teenagers 33
    Displaced Babies 39
Creating a Therapeutic Environment 43
    Satisfying the need for food 45
    Struggling to restore health 49
    Individual clothing styles and self-esteem 53
    Survivors cling to each other 57
    Babies need individual care 59
    Easing the young people's hearts 64
    Identifying the Children 75
    Searching for relatives who might have survived 83
Conflicts 90
    How much educational guidance is needed? 90
    Suddenly discovering sexuality 95
    Clashes with the German neighborhood 98
    Should survivors help with housework? 101
    Should Jews and Gentiles be separated? 103
Education and Leisure 110
    General education 110
    Vocational training 115
    Leisure activities 117
The Children's Center Changes 122

Significant fluctuations 124
Attempting to plan for the future.. 138
Repatriating Gentile children and teenagers 145
Moving the International D.P. Children's Center
from Kloster Indersdorf to Prien on Chiemsee 148
The Jewish Children's Center Kloster Indersdorf,
August 1946 to September 1948 154

Learning to Live with the Aftermath 159
And How Life Went On … 162
Greta Fischer – Stages in a Life................................. 172
Resources and Works Cited.. 180
Archives 180
Newspapers 180
Films... 181
Books.. 181
Illustrations.. 184

About the Author 186
Notes.. 187

Preface

Every year in July, dozens of senior men and women from around the world return to Germany. They have accepted an invitation from the concentration camp memorial at Flossenbürg, and their motives to come vary. They set out on the arduous journey to mourn their murdered family members, friends and comrades. They travel for the sake of finding traces of their own suffering, looking for graves and for those still missing. They come out of a sense of personal or family responsibility, from political conviction or psychological necessity.

Participants are getting on in years, the youngest among them today in their late seventies or early eighties. As children or teenagers they managed to escape the clutches of the National Socialist concentration camp system. Driven along on one of the most notorious death marches, they were liberated literally in the very last minutes before it was too late for them. They had survived systematic murder by the National Socialist regime, most often the only members of their families to have done so.

Martin Hecht was only 14 when he survived Flossenbürg concentration camp. Here he is next to his picture from Kloster Indersdorf on display at the Flossenbürg memorial site 2011.

In May 1945, these twelve- to fifteen-year-old children found themselves in a dramatic situation. The end of their imprisonment in camps meant far more than a mere liberation; it propelled them into a full realization of their loss. They had been robbed of all their family and social relationships. Their parents and relatives had been murdered; their childhood homes had ceased to exist. The experience of absolute vulnerability had had such a profound and shocking influence on them that normal social roles were turned upside down. As a result of living in permanent fear of death – a terror from which their parents had been unable to protect them – they had lost every shred of trust in the world of adults. In the camps, these youngsters had been painfully forced to fend for themselves if they were to survive. Survival had consumed all their energy. In terms of their psychological development, they stood on the threshold of puberty while disoriented and in extreme need of care. Given their experiences, however, they were no longer really children or youths.

For the Allied troops, the military government, and international charities, taking care of these young concentration camp survivors posed a challenge hitherto unknown. First, adequate housing and sufficient food had to be provided. The United Nations refugee organization UNRRA established children's centers and tried to meet the humanitarian and pedagogical challenge. Now that they were sheltered and cared for, the young people were encouraged to leave the camps behind them and to regain a life appropriate to their age. They were compelled to literally rediscover their real names, relearn basic social roles and gradually place an increasing trust in adults.

In this book, Anna Andlauer describes the history of the UNRRA Children's Center at Indersdorf. The story, however, encompasses far more than local historiography. From the start, the author was interested in the lives of the young camp survivors and their thorny paths back to "normal" living. She began a systematic search for the "Boys" of Indersdorf and discovered along the way far more than she had at first expected. Her meeting with them confronted her with history and narrative, trauma, hope, and survival. Research for this book made Anna Andlauer not merely an explorer, but a social worker, counselor and friend of the "Boys," now quite advanced in years.

These roles have been decisive for both the structure and style of the book. The author is an empathetic listener and an equally empathetic writer. In dense descriptions Anna Andlauer repeatedly allows her emotions to emerge; she approaches the feelings and sensations of these youths, and this permits her to convincingly portray their former survivors' worlds.

She reconstructs the individuality of these former teenagers, today's eighty-year-olds. This constitutes the book's humanizing achievement.

The study also honors the undeservedly obscure social worker Greta Fischer who, with others, cared for the young survivors and after whom a school in Dachau is named – this dedication, too, to the author's credit. The story of the "Boys" has now been told by Anna Andlauer. And we can't thank her enough.

Flossenbürg, March 2011
Jörg Skriebeleit

Foreword

"It was astonishing to see what a miracle could be worked for children orphaned by the Holocaust when the right thing was done,"[1] Greta Fischer discovered. She was one of the social workers on a UN team that set to work in Bavaria's Kloster Indersdorf to receive and help displaced children and youths. Here in an old monastery not far from Dachau in July 1945 the first international children's center in the American Zone in Germany was set up, an orphanage where Jewish and Gentile children and teenagers of various nationalities were cared for together, including those liberated from concentration camps, former forced laborers, and children of forced laborers — young people who had survived the horrors of the Second World War and the Holocaust and who had to be helped back on the road to life.

These young people had endured so much in the previous months and years, their suffering having been not only physical, but also, and even more important, psychological. They were devastated and highly disturbed. They had lost their next of kin, been removed from environments they could trust, and been forced to witness incomprehensible horror. All this left indelible marks on their souls.

In what state were these young, neglected, traumatized youths after liberation? What needed to be done to help them in the short and long term?

It was of course impossible to effect a real rehabilitation of young victims of National Socialism within six months or a year. Nonetheless, in the first three months after liberation, significant strides were made.

Hans Keilson, who researched long-term effects of persecution, recognized that what occurred immediately following the war would have a decisive influence on survivors' later lives: "Above all, I realized the meaning of the period immediately following the war as the children became aware of their fate and the help they were able to receive or miss out on during this important period."[2]

Participants in the Indersdorf Survivors' Meeting in front of a picture of Greta Fischer in July 2008. (from left) Hans Neumann, Erwin Farkas, Martin Hecht, Abram Leder, Eva Hahn, Walter Hahn, Zoltán Farkas, Michael V. Roth.

For the sake of research as well as human relationships, it is especially remarkable that in recent years more than fifty former residents of this children's center could be found: in the USA, Canada, Brazil, England, Belgium, Poland, France and Israel. Today, more than sixty years later, they are returning to visit "their" Kloster Indersdorf. They look back over the many years that have gone by, their childhoods, their youth during the Holocaust and how things went for them afterward. In the meantime, they remain eyewitnesses who have managed to live their daily lives in vastly different environments surprisingly well despite profound trauma.

These observations – even if valid for only a portion of those cared for at the time – lead to the question, what were the qualities and resources necessary to help these children regain their physical and mental health despite conditions immediately after the war?

Greta Fischer, the major chronicler of events, was in the midst of the action as she put her schooled therapist's eye to work in writing about her experiences. In the beginning of 1946 she penned a 33-page report about her UNRRA team's work with these "lost children of Europe."[3] Similarly, when later employed in Canada, Morocco, and Israel, she sought ways to promote her work with these young Holocaust survivors.[4] She constantly insisted that "the story of the children from Kloster Indersdorf must be told — their will to survive, their indescribable rage to live."[5] In her experience with these traumatized youngsters, she saw above all "proof of the resilience of people and the indomitable courage of the human spirit."[6]

In the 1980s, Greta Fischer stood again in front of the door of Kloster Indersdorf to see once more her former workplace. But because the old Bavarian convent now housed a lively school, and since hardly anyone present there knew anything about the place in the immediate postwar years, she was sadly denied entry. In December 1986, fewer than two years before her death, she wrote to her friend Esther Halevi that, since she had seen the film *Shoah*, she had become even more firmly convinced that the story had to be told. But how, she wondered, admitting that she nearly phoned Elie Wiesel, whom she had met in Toronto, for help.[7]

Following her aunt's sudden death in 1988, Lilo Plasches found among Fischer's papers reports of Indersdorf and many unique historical photos — expression of the unfulfilled desire to let the world know about her experiences with the youngest of Nazi victims. This book serves to convey some of the story Greta Fischer wished to tell. The text is based on her writings as well as a video interview from 1985. Documents housed in various archives (above all the United Nations Archives) letters and a report from the nuns employed in the convent and especially the survivors' memories flesh out the picture. Much of what was found, even items of seeming insignificance, speak for themselves, detailing daily life in postwar Kloster Indersdorf and, hopefully, helping to open the doors to former residents who have made return visits from all corners of the globe.

Only since the mid-eighties has German historiography concerned itself with Jewish DPs; it took even longer before attention was paid to the special situation of the youngest victims in numerous children's centers, [8] despite the fact that the fate of the children is mentioned in nearly all publications on the history of Jewish DPs.[9] Here we should mention the seminal studies, Juliane Wetzel's *Jüdisches Leben in München 1945-51. Durchgangsstation oder Wiederaufbau?* (1987) and Jaqueline D. Giere's dissertation, *Wir sind unterwegs, aber nicht in der Wüste. Erziehung und Kultur in den jüdischen Displaced Persons Lagern der Amerikanischen Zone im Nachkriegsdeutschland 1945-1949* (1993).

This pioneer research notwithstanding, the many efforts to begin life anew in Germany after the war – and to renew daily life in children's camps in particular – have not received systematic attention.[10]

The first comprehensive book to address a broad public on this issue appeared in 1994, Angelika Königseder and Juliane Wetzel's *Lebensmut im Wartesaal: Die jüdischen DPs (Displaced Persons) im Nachkriegsdeutschland*. It mentions Indersdorf for the first time as an international children's center and later a Jewish orphanage.

Then in 2006, Jim G. Tobias and Nicola Schlichting gave a chapter to the Indersdorf children's center in their book *Heimat auf Zeit. Jüdische Kinder in Rosenheim 1946-47*.

This study continues the research begun by Königseder, Wetzel, Tobias and Schlichting and describes the first year in operation of the "International D.P. Children's Center Kloster Indersdorf." What requires further research is the dramatic change in daily life once the center became an orphanage exclusively for Jewish children (August 1946 – September 1948).

Even though I have lived for more than twenty years near Dachau and have been engaged in historical research, I was largely unaware of the story of postwar Kloster Indersdorf. I have Eleonore Philipp to thank for bringing this topic to my attention. I discovered Greta Fischer's report in the archive of the Heimatverein — a local historical association — of Indersdorf. As a teacher at Markt Indersdorf high school, I assigned a student to delve further into the report and soon recognized the unique value of this historical document. Since then I have been on an exciting voyage of discovery. In archives all over the world I found photographs and documents and exhibited them in Indersdorf, Recklinghausen and Jerusalem. My research first appeared in *Nach der »Stunde Null«. Stadt und Landkreis Dachau 1945 bis 1949*[11] and in the 2010 Yearbook of the Nürnberger Institut für NS-Forschung und jüdische Geschichte des 20. Jahrhunderts [Nuremberg Institute for Research on National Socialism and Jewish History of the Twentieth Century].[12] A traveling exhibition intended for display primarily in Central and Eastern Europe will hopefully encourage even more former center dwellers to come forward and return to their earlier residence. We were able to trace many former child survivors to Israel and above all to the English-speaking world; they are happy to be invited with their families to see Indersdorf again, to renew acquaintance with one another after 60 years and to make new friends. For the time being, a climax of this development has been the naming of a school in Dachau after Greta Fischer in 2011, inspired by the spirit of her work.

Participants in the Indersdorf reunion 2011 were interviewed as experts on "resilience" at the Greta-Fischer-Schule Dachau. (1st row from left) Jack Terry, Leslie Kleinman, Eric Hitter, Martin Hecht, Gisèle Niango, Steve Israeler (2nd row) Walter Beausert, Susanne Urban (ITS), Anna Andlauer (Author), Margret Schlenke (ITS), Daniel Baumann

The State of Bavaria and the Concentration Camp Memorial at Flossenbürg have been inviting survivors annually since 1995 to Flossenbürg (in northern Bavaria) – a significant gesture in contemporary memorial efforts. Even after 65 years, 60 former prisoners from all over the world, accompanied by 300 family members, have accepted the invitation. These annual gatherings have permitted me to invite those who had been cared for in Indersdorf to revisit "their" center and participate in discussions with peers, to enjoy celebrations and go on day excursions. A ZDF (TV) film *Aus der Hölle ins Leben* [From Hell Back to Life] documented these events.[13]

I thank all the survivors for their moving stories, photos and documents that became a part of this book, directly or indirectly. I'm grateful for their many expressions of friendship and hope that I've done them justice in this work.

For generous financial support, without which this project would not have been possible, my special thanks go to the Stiftung Bayerische Gedenkstätten (Foundation for Bavarian Memorials), the Bayerische Landeszentrale für politische Bildungsarbeit, the Foundation "Erinnerung, Verantwortung und Zukunft," the BMW Group, the Sisters of Mercy of Saint Vincent de Paul, to the Patton Plusczyk Foundation, to the district of Upper Bavaria, to Dachau county, to the community of Indersdorf, the Bürgerstiftung Markt Indersdorf, the Stiftung der Sparkasse Dachau, the Heimatverein (historical association), and the Indersdorf VHS (community college). Very special thanks go to Jörg Skriebeleit and the team of the Flossenbürg Memorial, Dr. Susanne Urban of the International Tracing Service in Bad Arolsen, Jude Richter of the US Holocaust Memorial Museum in Washington D.C., the teaching staff of the school Vinzenz von Paul and the Greta-Fischer-Schule, and last but not least, all the enthusiastic supporters of our Indersdorf project: Inge Künzner, Angelika Eisenmann, Hanni Norgauer, Gottfried Biesemann, Verena Buser and my husband Jörg.

A hearty thanks goes to the relatives and friends of Greta Fischer in Israel, England, Canada and Switzerland, especially Micha Plaschkes, Hanna Corbishley and Fraidie Martz, who were so generous with photos, documents and personal memories which enriched this book. Tobe Levin has translated the German edition of this book into English. Thanks to her *Zurück ins Leben. Das internationale Kinderzentrum Kloster Indersdorf 1945-46* has become *The Rage to Live. The International D.P. Children's Center Kloster Indersdorf 1945-46*. I also take pleasure in thanking Tobe Levin and Diana Morris-Bauer who invested considerable energy in proofing the text and contributing their advice and expertise in matters of style and content. Their suggestions have made this a better read. My special thanks go as well to Nicola Schlichting and Jim G. Tobias of the Nuremberg Institute for Research on National Socialism and Jewish History of the Twentieth Century whose constructive engagement, critical commentary, advice about the structure of the study as well as expertise, accompanied me patiently while I wrote. Naturally, mistakes may have crept in for which I alone am responsible. Errors of course may occur but I have done my very best to come as close to the historical truth as possible.

Weichs, April 2012
Anna Andlauer

Help for Survivors

On May 8, 1945, the war ended on the European front. Twelve years of National Socialist rule had left widespread material, human and moral devastation and a Europe on the brink of utter chaos. Among millions of refugees were those liberated from concentration and labor camps as well as those who had survived the Nazi dictatorship in hiding or by using a false identity. To answer the immediate needs of these abducted, homeless and uprooted people, called Displaced Persons (DPs), food, clothing and medicine had to be supplied. To manage this task, the Allies in their respective occupation zones constructed so-called DP camps. These sprang up wherever the necessary infrastructure could be found: in former concentration camps, in barracks that had served the army or SS, in hotels, monasteries or private homes.[14] In the mid-forties, the Allies had already anticipated dealing with innumerable prisoners and forced laborers after liberation,[15] and in November 1943 the United Nations Relief and Rehabilitation Administration (UNRRA)[16] was founded. The UNRRA teams were attached to various military divisions and followed the fighting troops in order to support the military in caring for the millions of victims and preparing for their expected repatriation. Given the extreme destruction wrought by World War II, these tasks appeared larger than ever before but demanded a speedy response.

With only a vague idea of what awaited her, thirty-five-year-old social worker Greta Fischer[17] arrived in Germany in June 1945 with UNRRA Team 182. "There was no order of the day. Everything was kind of spontaneous. And there was [great] confusion in Germany also. Soldiers coming back from the war, other soldiers coming to help in the liberation ...."[18] Fischer was especially worried about the "unaccompanied children," the young, including teenagers, who were left to wander without their parents or other adult companionship.[19] "Homeless, emaciated, covered with scars, fearful, bitter victims of robbery, witnesses of horrors – those were the children of liberated Europe."[20] "Lost children" Greta Fischer called these young foreigners as they crisscrossed postwar Germany in ceaseless search of relatives and food, asking how and if they would be able to move on with their lives.[21] In order to funnel aid directly to these victims, the UNRRA Team 182 and Greta Fischer were charged with creating a refugee center for young survivors to provide once again a protective environment. "It was recommended that the center be located outside but within reasonable distance from Munich since ... problems peculiar to a children's institution [were anticipated] which would require frequent consultations with representatives of the Third Army Headquarters,"[22] Greta Fischer wrote. In this situation nobody knew what to expect; nobody anticipated how great the need would be, nor the nationalities or ages of the uprooted children.[23] The G5 department of the 3rd US Army, responsible for DPs, estimated that in its area alone, there would be 7,000 children.[24] For instance, in Munich UNRRA workers discovered more than 50 small children in private homes or public buildings.[25] The Feldafing camp housed 400 teens while in Traunstein 249 foreign children were on the road, at times with their teachers.[26] These uprooted youngsters could be found everywhere, and they needed immediate aid.

Meeting of UNRRA Team 182. (from left) Marion E. Hutton, director Lillian D. Robbins, André Marx, Dr. Gaston Gérard, Harry C. Parker, Greta Fischer, Helen Steiger, unidentified.

The "International D.P. Children's Center Kloster Indersdorf" opens its doors

A mere fifteen kilometers from the recently liberated Dachau concentration camp in a small Bavarian village, UNRRA volunteers found the old convent Kloster Indersdorf[27] on June 25, 1945. The inner chapel dated from the twelfth century, whereas the rest of the structure had been renovated and expanded by Augustinians in the eighteenth century. For sixty years, the Sisters of Mercy of Saint Vincent de Paul had run an orphanage there until the nuns were expelled by the Nazis. During the war, the large building housed the Bavarian Agency for the Homeless[28] which provided "compulsory care for homeless youths."[29]

Aerial photo of Kloster Indersdorf in the 1950s.

Here basic equipment could be found, making it feasible to open a children's center quickly. Within days, the U.S. Army took possession of the old building and handed it over to UNRRA Team 182 on July 7. Fifteen of the children who were already there simply remained because it was presumed they were foreign-born. Twenty more children whom the UNRRA team had discovered in Munich would follow on August 4.[30]

At first glance, the centuries-old convent had seemed appropriate as a refuge for children; up to twenty-five young people could be accommodated in dormitories with beds. There were leisure areas; a large, central, elegant Baroque hall became the dining hall; a well-equipped kitchen was quite conveniently attached. The "Cloister"[31] had a gymnasium, lavatories and workshops. It also had its own farm with eleven cows, some 30 pigs, four horses, about 240 hens, fields for crops, and well-kept vegetable and flower gardens which suggested the residents would be able to at least partially supply their own food.[32] A second glance, however, revealed the disadvantages of an ancient building: it could not provide hot running water, and the long corridors were uncomfortably drafty. Nonetheless, because hospitals and sanatoria for the wounded were over-booked, the big building would have to do for the time being while better housing was sought.[33]

Indersdorf was a pioneer project[34] served by eleven and later seventeen highly motivated and dedicated UNRRA volunteers from all over the world.[35] The main eyewitness of events, Greta Fischer, wrote: "We started with the United Nation's team, which was an international team, which were all professionals, professional people, I would say, very special people, each one in professional know-how and also in devotion, resourcefulness and commitment to the cause."[36]

The first director of UNRRA Team 182 was the experienced social worker Lillian D. Robbins. She was replaced in early 1946 by Canadian Jean Margaret Henshaw.[37] A social worker's duties included looking after the children's physical and psychological well-being, seeing to their education, searching for family members and starting the emigration or repatriation process. The vice-director, American Marion E. Hutton, was responsible for registering the children. As Welfare and Principal Welfare Officer,

André Marx and Greta Fischer were chosen. Marx was a Jewish survivor from Luxembourg[38] responsible for planning the school curriculum. "He is the light of our ethical lives; for our education alone, he strives," as one Jewish survivor rhymed about him.[39]

UNRRA Team 182: (1st row from left) Harry C. Parker, Greta Fischer, unidentified, Helen Steiger, Lillian D. Robbins, unidentified, André Marx, Marion E. Hutton. (2nd row) John Gower, Dr. Gaston Gérard, Yvonne Menny, Josef Conrady, two French drivers.

Greta Fischer's duties consisted at first of securing optimal care for the youngest victims, as well as training and supervising personnel. Starting in the fall of 1945, she became responsible for planning the entire program. Helen Steiger, a Swiss teacher, was assigned to help the child survivors to find their families. French nurse Yvonne Menny gave a helping hand to Belgian medical officer Gaston Gérard. Australian Edna Davis, engaged as a nurse, was also assigned to clothing distribution and to teach English. Englishmen John Gower and Harry C. Parker were Supply and Warehouse Officers for the procurement and administration of supplies. Josef Conrady from Luxembourg served as head cook. In the fall of 1945, Miss Tillmann took charge of leisure activities while Anna Marie de Waal-Malefyt from the Netherlands was engaged as a medical social worker.[40] All volunteers needed many skills. For instance, the cook was expected not only to provide meals for hundreds every day, but also to know about special dietary requirements. The two French drivers had not only to transport supplies, but also to make contact with the children and talk to them.[41] To house the UNRRA personnel, the US Army requisitioned the finest houses in the village; some volunteers, however, like Greta Fischer, preferred to live in the cloister together with those they were caring for.

Helpers in the Pioneer Project

When opening the Children's Center, the volunteers faced serious challenges. While the building was being cleaned and supplies stored, the first small children and youngsters had already arrived. At first the UNRRA team expected the old convent to house 75 to 100 children[42] who would be speedily repatriated to their home countries. However, on September 15, 1945, 192 boys and girls from 13 different nations, including 49 Jews had already moved in.[43] These children needed not only food, clothing, clean beds, warm baths and medical care, but also psychological counseling, education and leisure activities. Organizing all of this exceeded the resources of the eleven-member UNRRA team.

For that reason, efforts were made at once to induce the Sisters of Mercy to return to Indersdorf. On opening day, July 11, 1945, the first Sisters arrived after a seven-year absence. The villagers and the UNRRA Team greeted them warmly and were quite content when the nuns set about assigning themselves rooms.[44]

The Sisters were put to work on the farm and in the kitchen, the laundry and the sewing workshop; as experienced nursery school teachers, Adelgunde Flierl and Audakta Huber were ideal for the little ones. The nuns were treated by the UNRRA team in a "friendly, helpful, tactful and courteous manner," head nun M. Dolorosa Mayer wrote. Her letters to their motherhouse in Munich describe the work: "We have to clean and set up the place as quickly as possible, but my hands are tied because I'm told to do too much at the same time. For example, we need to clean and furnish a huge area to store everything ordered for the house.

Mother Superior Dolorosa Mayer (in black) with the Sisters of Mercy of Saint Vincent de Paul, 1945.

It's not easy."[45] Nonetheless, the Sisters took up their assigned tasks with enthusiasm and devotion. "Yesterday Sister M. Ado tackled a whole mountain of laundry. Unfortunately, the washing machines are broken. Not a single one can be used. It was really tedious. She had no soap, no brushes, and hardly any washing powder; and yet, she did it! As for Sister M. Audakta, she's with the children. ... Sister M. Adelgunde really had her hands full trying to get everything done that she'd been assigned. Yesterday, for instance, she had to deal with two whole truckloads of kitchen things, bedding and material; every day brings something similar."[46] The Sisters' management of the center proved to be remarkably focused and energetic; the UNRRA team considered them a loyal and hard-working staff, as Greta Fischer noted forty years later, still full of praise: "The nuns [there] to help us were really wonderful people."[47]

If the young survivors were to be well cared for, and especially in light of general scarcity, the center had to turn itself into a productive unit, a stressful and demanding task. The fields and vegetable gardens had to be tended with the most primitive tools; pails were used to carry hot water for bathing and cleaning; the ovens had to be managed by hand; the walls needed paint, and floors and corridors wanted repair. There was a shoe repair workshop for refurbishing and sometimes making the children's footwear from scratch; clothing had to be sewn, and the center's own butcher worked overtime.

Of the earlier German personnel who had been employed at the Indersdorf children's center, only one girl for the kitchen, a seamstress, a maid, and the secretary, Centa Probstmayr, would see their employment renewed. The latter had been working at the center since 1941 and at times had been solely responsible for managing the entire institution.

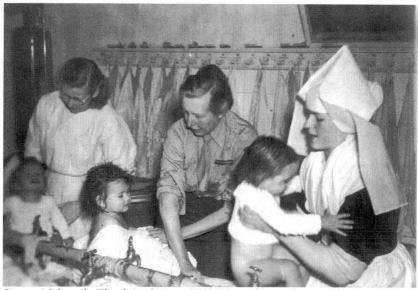

Sister Adelgunde Flierl (right), an UNRRA worker and an adult DP with toddlers in the convent bathroom.

To overcome the lack of workers, in July 1945, ten farmhands, six gardeners, five seamstresses, three washerwomen, eight kitchen help, fourteen housemaids, a nurse, three nurse's assistants, a guard, a handyman, two office staff and a custodian were hired.[48] Most were German refugees from East Prussia or Silesia who received not only wages, but also housing and food. The Sisters didn't always have it easy trying to organize and manage these German workers laboring in such a large building and in the fields. Sister Dolorosa, for instance, kept an eye out to ensure that all the milk was actually delivered to the Children's Center, since the staff was not without reproach: "We're having a real hard time with these girls. The two worst cases have been dismissed. They came home at 11:30 at night with two drunken soldiers. And others run off to be with the Americans every night. We have only five left."[49] The UNRRA's inspection team report expressly recommended in November 1945 that a supervisor for the cleaning staff be appointed.[50]

The hiring of German personnel ensured the center's economic functioning, but even more urgent was the question of care. Who could be entrusted with direct interaction with the youths? Understandably, this task could not be given to Germans.[51] Yet members of the UNRRA Team 182 were unable to master this immense assignment on their own. Due to UNRRA guidelines, the number of caretakers could not exceed 5% of the number cared for, which meant that personnel in Indersdorf were on duty day and night: "My memory goes back to many nights looking after 25-30 babies who demanded to be fed and comforted, trying to snatch a couple of hours of sleep in-between."[52] As increasing numbers of "unaccompanied children" arrived at Indersdorf, their numbers having reached more than 300 in the meantime, the striking lack of employees grew unbearable. Adult DPs were therefore tasked with helping the child survivors as house parents and teachers since they, too, had endured similar experiences and came from the same cultures. The aim was to have one adult for five or six kids. "We engaged displaced persons of all the different nationalities we had in order ... that the children were cared for individually and could speak their own languages."[53]

It wasn't easy, however, to find qualified personnel in the ranks of the other DPs, quite simply because "many of the best professional leaders of the Allied countries [had] been exterminated."[54] Adults DPs were also in want of aid, had been marked by their own persecution or internment in camps and were emotionally unstable. Greta Fischer points out that they were often wholly consumed by their own repatriation issues, involved in political disputes or more interested in satisfying their own needs than in overseeing young people's development. However, housing in bedrooms for two or three and payment in kind with cigarettes, chocolate, "fine soap" and clothing was enticing.[55] Despite a few praiseworthy exceptions, such as the dentist Dr. Josef Unger, most grown-up DPs came to the center for the better care, or at least so it seemed to the Sisters of Mercy.[56]

A session at the bath with UNRRA child specialist Greta Fischer in May 1946.

In the meantime, 94 adult DPs had taken up residence in the house – a number far exceeding the guidelines issued by the UNRRA. In November 1945 an UNRRA screening team even came to the hard conclusion that not only did "a large percentage" of grown-up DPs offer "no value for the children," but even worse, that "their presence disturbs the atmosphere in the home."[57] Some adults DPs therefore had to be sent away; others had their DP status cancelled[58] while still others allowed themselves to be repatriated at a time when these individuals were still urgently needed in the children's center.

Thus, again and again we find numerous reasons for the lack of reliable teachers as well as resident foster "parents." What's more, tensions between German and foreign helpers made it hard to retain or hire German personnel, strains that even broke out in isolated incidents of violence. As a result, the situation found relief only once organizations like the Polish and French Red Cross[59] sent volunteers and teachers. Some of those assigned in this way, like Dr. Martha Branscombe[60] from the US Committee for European Children, were considered as full-fledged members of the UNRRA Team and given tasks as social workers.

Displaced Children arrive

By June 12, 1946, more than 6,000 foreign children, who were without parents or other relatives, had been registered in the US occupation zone. About 2,000 had been found by UNRRA search teams. The others had been discovered in DP camps together with adults or had been noticed by chance by the US Army or UNRRA because they huddled together in groups and generally appeared to be in a pitiful condition. The Jewish displaced children were mainly survivors of concentration camps. Among the Gentile displaced children, a distinction existed, however. In the western part of the US Zone there were mainly teenagers who, as a result of individual tragedies such as "accidental separation from the parent, death of the parent or abandonment," had been housed in German establishments; in the eastern part, in Bavaria, large groups of children and youths were found who had been "violently removed from their homes" and "brought back from Eastern European countries." The children who described "forcible removal from their homes and admission to institutions where no language other than German was permitted" chiefly came from the Upper Silesia area.[61] In the Bavarian region around Regensburg, Traunstein and Straubing, a significant number of such Upper Silesians were found. Even if many of these children and teenagers considered themselves to be Germans, immediately after the war they had to pretend to be Polish in order to be reunited with their families, as Upper Silesia had become a part of Poland again. Because in summer of 1945 no one had any idea of how large the need was, the UNRRA Team 182 was mandated to assist every non-German orphan found in the territory overseen by the UN. As a result, things got off to "an uncontrolled start,"[62] when the heavy doors of the convent were thrown open to the displaced children in southern Germany.

The numbers of those demanding admission to the Indersdorf Children's Center were high: "Since Monday children have been arriving daily. The first group consisted of 10 boys from 14-17 years, Hungarian Jews. That already sent us into shock. Then on Tuesday 25 Polish kids arrived, from tiny two-month-olds to two-year-olds and some girls and boys up to 16. On Wednesday, nine more little ones ... and yesterday again seven bigger girls with scabies — totally neglected. I simply can't see how we're going to manage with 200 kids like that without the proper supervision and instruction. On the first day the boys had already taken the horses from the stable and [ridden] away. ... Tomorrow 35 Poles are due to arrive; I think boys and girls."[63]

A group of Jewish survivors. (2nd row from left) Ignaz Niedermann, Lazar Fürst, two unidentified, Abram Leder, Bernat Niedermann; (1st row) Szlama Weichselblatt, Herbert Hahn, unidentified, Walter Hahn.

Already on August 3, 1945, the unimaginable number of 200 children, youths and young adults had been reached, and the "wild," "undisciplined" behavior of the "children" (up to 25 years old) had thrown the home into a "terrible condition," as the Sisters saw it.[64] Nonetheless, they fought courageously with other volunteers to ensure that arrivals received the most essential care.

Two months after Kloster Indersdorf had opened, employees were briefed by an Allied Expert Group on the psychological problems to be expected from the repatriation of DPs.[65] Yet at this point in time, the UNRRA volunteers had already experienced dealing with nearly 200 troubled little children, teens and young adults of various backgrounds and languages and had formed their own opinions regarding how these "displaced" or "unaccompanied children" were best to be helped.

During the one year of International D.P. Children's Center Kloster Indersdorf's existence, the number of "bigger children" varied greatly. The first nine months saw an average population of between 180 and 200 youths and young adults to care for. That number rose in the last months to 220 to 240.[66] In the early months, there had been between 30 and 50 small children; in March-April 1946, the number rose to 60, and by the time of the move to Prien on Chiemsee in July-August 1946, Indersdorf reached its peak of 76 small children.[67]

Jewish child survivors

Because Jewish children had been direct targets of the Nazi genocide, Indersdorf housed hardly any Jewish boys or girls under age twelve. Jewish arrivals tended to be young people[68] between twelve and twenty-five and generally male. They came almost exclusively from Poland, Hungary or the borderlands then belonging to Hungary, with a few from the Soviet Union.[69] Since 1939, Jewish Poles had been exposed to Nazi terror that led in 1940 to internment in the ghetto and, in most cases, to deportation of their families to extermination camps as well. A similar fate awaited the Soviet and Baltic Jews once they were taken by surprise when Germany invaded the Soviet Union in 1941, while the Jews in Hungary were sharply persecuted "only" since 1944. Nearly all the child survivors who showed up at Indersdorf had been separated from their families on the selection platforms of extermination camps, mainly Auschwitz. They had been "permitted" to remain alive, for the time being, and escape "selection" by claiming to be older. With considerable luck and an iron will to live they somehow got through as slave laborers in various camps.

They had been put to work under conditions as punishing as those of adults in factories, quarries, as well as road and railway construction. Like grown-ups, they too had had to stand "Appell" and suffered the same hunger, cold, illness, violence and exposure to death. As the Soviet troops drew nearer, they were driven on death marches or shipped off to more western camps in cattle wagons. Some were liberated in Mauthausen, Buchenwald, Dachau or Bergen-Belsen, and a few individuals from Terezin; most however had last been captives in the Flossenbürg concentration camp and were on a death march toward Dachau when General Patton's troops liberated them on April 23, 1945, near Stamsried (north-eastern Bavaria).[70]

Jakob Hecht was from Romania and Nelly Jussem from Austria, both 15 years old.

The young people had gone through inconceivable horrors. Often they were the only survivors of their families, even if at this moment they were not yet aware of this and held tight to the hope of finding at least one or two of their close relatives.[71]

In her report Greta Fischer describes the parallels and differences in various histories of persecution, for instance the fate of Abram Warszaw. As a thirteen-year-old, together with his nine-year-old brother Laib, he escaped from the Kozienice Ghetto in Poland at his father's behest. For three months the boys wandered around in the woods, slept in haystacks and barns, and lived like wild, panicked animals. Yes, they had known poverty and hunger from before, but conditions now overpowered them. Realizing they just couldn't take it anymore, they joined a Jewish prisoners' work commando. Abram, whose greatest aim was to get his brother through unharmed, had to watch as Laib was shot and killed by the SS. He was then interned in many concentration camps, and as the Soviet troops approached, was even sent to Mauthausen in upper Austria. After being liberated, Abram lived with a group of twelve young survivors for a couple of weeks in a house in Regensburg until he met a Canadian UNRRA worker in the street who took him to Indersdorf.[72]

Abram Warszaw survived Mauthausen concentration camp while Miklos Roth was rescued the very last minute when Flossenbürg concentration camp was finally liberated.

In contrast to Abram, a few of the Jewish youths had survived arrest and forced labor because they had taken Aryan names and had been living with Christian families – like Janek, for example. His parents, two brothers and a sister had been killed in the Warsaw Ghetto. Janek fled and was able to survive in Warsaw under a false name. In August 1944 he succeeded in reaching Upper Silesia where the arrival of Soviet troops early in 1945 made it possible for him to emerge from hiding. A Jewish friend brought him to Germany where the American Army delivered him to Indersdorf.[73]

Kurt Klappholz survived 14 different concentration camps while Hans Neumann suffered in Terezin for three years. Both were the only survivors of their families.

In Kloster Indersdorf, Greta Fischer learned first-hand about the many and various forms of persecution, well before the full extent of Nazi cruelties had been broadly revealed. Take, for instance, fifteen-year-old Halina Bryks. Following the murder of her parents, she worked in the kitchen and in construction at Markstädt-Fünfeichen concentration camp[74] and, toward the end, for twelve hours a day in a munitions factory. After liberation by the Soviet Army, she fought her way back to her hometown in Orkusz near Krakow. The anti-Semitism of her Polish neighbors rapidly convinced her to move away again. With her cousin she went to Weiden in northern Bavaria and from there to Indersdorf.[75]

The Hungarian Jew Miklos Roth was only thirteen when, on a death march, he witnessed the murder of his father, who, unable to walk any further, was shot right outside the gates of Buchenwald; Miklos himself belonged to the thousands of deathly ill who were found in Flossenbürg on April 23, 1945, by the Third US Army as they reached this concentration camp.[76]

The Hahn brothers from Vienna survived three years in Terezin together with Hans Neumann from Berlin.

Starting in 1942, Kurt Klappholz suffered through fourteen different camps. He became the spokesman for a group of about twenty Jewish youngsters who knew each other from the camps or had met after liberation in Neunburg vorm Wald (northern Bavaria). Salek (Israel) Benedikt[77] was one of them, as were Imre Hitter and the Weinstock brothers. All had been interned in labor camps and forced to work under inhuman conditions, and at the end of the war, they had survived the extreme overcrowding of the Flossenbürg camp. Alfred Buchführer gave an eyewitness account of how hundreds of fellow prisoners had been killed when they were forced to march in rain and cold weather and without any food.[78] Only at the last minute were they snatched by the Americans from the death march toward Dachau, as Klappholz described it fifty years later: "Had they come two or three days later, you wouldn't be speaking to me now."[79] Finally, at the end of August 1945, the group arrived at Indersdorf where they were welcomed by the director, Lillian D. Robbins, who "made a welcoming speech and set [the boys] at ease."[80] For all, Kloster Indersdorf was "superb," as Kurt Klappholz later expressed.[81]

Another path brought the tall, blond Berliner Hans Neumann and two brothers from Vienna, Walter and Herbert Hahn, to Indersdorf. As "half Jews" they had been interned in Terezin, had been liberated by the Soviets on May 8, 1945, and made their own way to the convent. Because they spoke German, they first had to convince the Americans that they were indeed among the persecuted. In the DP camp Deggendorf, Neumann finally received recognition from an American official: "This boy is alone and has been with Walter and Herbert Hahn for the last three years. They would all like to stay together and I suggest that this should be done if at all possible."[82]

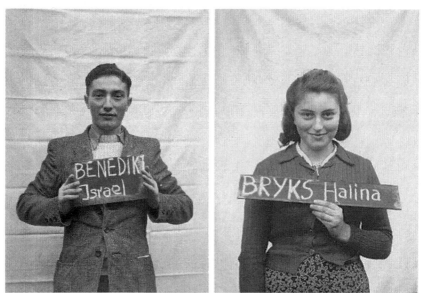

The Jewish survivors Salek Benedikt and Halina Bryks could not return to Poland because all their close family members were killed and their homes destroyed.

The lives of such youngsters as Halina, Miklos, Kurt or Hans had been threatened daily, even hourly. "Life became a day to day or even hourly gamble."[83] Now their most urgent desire was to find family and leave Germany as quickly as possible.

The UNRRA team quickly understood that their initial mandate, to repatriate all children, could not be fulfilled. The Jewish children in particular announced on arrival that under no circumstances would they want to return to their home nations. Instead "the Jewish children want desperately to leave Germany for a free country. They do not wish to return to their country of origin."[84] However, it was not yet known for sure that they had lost both parents and that no one was waiting for them where they had been living before.

The arrival of these children shocked the Sisters. They found them "wild" and "without restraint"; horrified by their behavior, they had little understanding for the fact that for years, these boys and girls had lived in hell, in an environment that had invalidated all ethical values and norms. And the nuns, with their strict Catholic morals, appeared to the survivors, given their experience, totally strange. Salek Benedikt, the 18-year-old concentration camp survivor, said, "The incumbent nuns went about their duties, unobtrusively, oblivious to the fact that we were Holocaust survivors."[85] Polish youths like Salek Benedikt had had their frightful experiences with "Christian brotherly love" as practiced by the Polish Catholic church. Greta Fischer could therefore empathize with those young people whose Jewish identity made it hard for them to accept being cared for by nuns. Moreover, it appeared that the Sisters' strict ideas concerning education were not wholly compatible with what UNRRA's volunteers had in mind.

Gentile teenagers

In addition to the large group of concentration camp survivors, Kloster Indersdorf received many non-Jewish youths. Some of them had also survived internment in concentration camps. For example, the Polish boy Zenon Zalewsky had survived Dachau concentration camp and his compatriot Zdzislaw Szymanek the even more notorious terror camp Mauthausen.[86]

Most, however, had been forced laborers from Central or Eastern European countries like Poland, Czechoslovakia and Yugoslavia, who had been "rounded up in the villages at the point of a gun and brought into Germany." They had worked on railroads, on farms, and in factories like Messerschmitt in Augsburg.[87]

Zdzislaw Szymanek survived Mauthausen concentration camp and Zenon Zalewski nearby Dachau concentration camp. Both Gentile boys returned to Poland in 1946.

Others were children of forced laborers or had been transported to Germany as part of the Germanization movement. And their histories of persecution were no less horrifying: "Though a very large number of them came to Kloster Indersdorf from concentration camps, we soon learned that many who had not seen these particular hell holes did not fare much better."[88] For instance, the young Soviet former forced laborer Alexander Orloff. With his mother dead and his father in the Red Army, Alexander had been left alone with his sister. As the Germans invaded his village near Kiev, he was discovered and brought as a slave laborer to Germany and Austria.[89] The twelve- and fifteen-year-old Serbian brothers Vlada and Zlatko Jovanovic, as well as their friend Milan Glaban, were shabby, hungry and dirty as they wandered from the British to the American Zone of Germany. In their first interview with UNRRA in Passau, the brothers told their story. Originally from Belgrade, they had been kidnapped and put to work on German farms. They had had to work hard, receiving for meals only a few potatoes and from time to time a little coffee and a slice of bread. The UNRRA attracted them to Indersdorf with the promise that they would be driven immediately back to Belgrade.[20]

Others among the child slave laborers, for instance the Czech youngster Franz Grimm, had been forced to join the German Army as Soviet troops drew near. Such was the case of Polish Zbigniew Gajewski. First brought to Germany and forced to work, he was assigned in April 1945 to the front where he was wounded before the Americans captured him. He was sent to an American prisoner-of-war camp, released in October and finally taken to Indersdorf.[21]

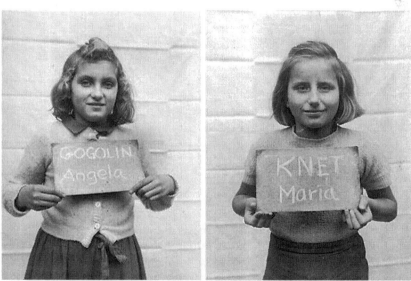

Angela and Maria wanted to return to eastern Upper Silesia, which had been Polish before the war, German during the war and became Polish again while the children were waiting.

Other children considered "racially suitable" as "Volksdeutsche" — Germans by blood — were therefore shipped to Germany from Yugoslavia, Czechoslovakia and, above all, from Upper Silesia.[92] An especially large number were found in Bavaria, 1,000 from Upper Silesia alone, as a study in April 1946 showed.[93] Many had been kidnapped, but with others this was questionable.

Regina Cierpiol (right) was 12 years old and her sister Martha 14 when waiting at Kloster Indersdorf to be reunited with their family in Upper Silesia.

For instance, two school classes totaling about 60 girls from Königshütte and Bismarckhütte (Chorzów) in Upper Silesia arrived in Indersdorf. In January 1945 they had been brought – under the pretext of taking a local class trip – by their German teachers to farms near Straubing (Bavaria) instead. As one of the girls, Ursula Weißmann, sees it, because Upper Silesia had a German-Polish population and during the war German was spoken both in schools and many parental homes, her group of unequivocally "German" girls had been brought to safety from the advancing Soviet troops. "Our parents had agreed and on the way, we even had to take the oath of the BDM.[24] The teachers who accompanied us, Frau Körner and Frau Binghard, were that dedicated to National Socialism."[25] Others, like Martha and Regina Cierpiol, considered themselves to be Polish and were sure that their parents had not wanted them to be taken to Germany.

However, their parents could have had no idea that they would be separated from their daughters for one and a half years and then, following the war, would be reunited with them –given changed political circumstances –only under the pretext of their being Polish, which allowed them to return to Upper Silesia.[26]

On farms in Rain, Bergsdorf and Wiesendorf near Straubing (Bavaria), these girls had performed menial labor.[27]

Only in mid-August 1945 were they discovered by a Polish liaison officer. He described the situation as follows:

At first sight, I gained the impression that those children were scared and worried. They seemed not to understand who was the person that came to see them and what was this person bringing them, what they were facing [sic]. Little by little I started to gain their confidence. They began to speak to me in Polish — chiefly old farmers' Polish — to confide to me their worries and woes, some of them little, others large. I noticed that the process of the Germanization of these children had reached in some cases an advanced stage. The years of compulsory German education, under the general terror of German occupation, was driving them along; as I observed many times, toward irresolution and real conflicts of infantine conscience. Nevertheless, there were still some children who had resisted. There was evidence of attachment to the familiar sounds of the mother tongue and very remote remembrances of the pre-war family hearth.[28]

The Polish liaison officer simply assumed that these girls' mother tongue and identity were Polish. He found twenty-four of these unhappy victims in a restaurant annex lying on old straw with filthy covers. They were exhausted, undernourished, and covered with scabies. The girls were offered immediate medical help, received milk, sugar, chocolate and soup, and soon most of them were on their way to Markt Indersdorf.[22]

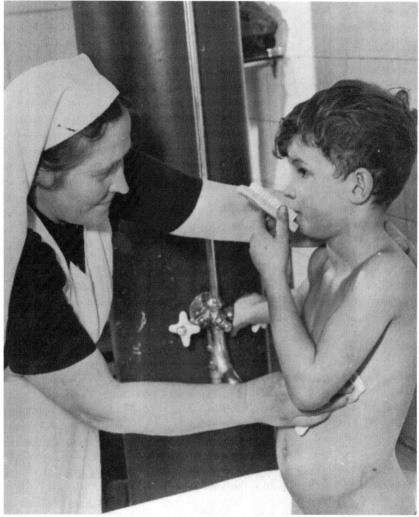

Paluojis Livi, a nurse from Estonia and herself a DP, ensures that Alexander Pecha is thoroughly scrubbed before medical examination.

Extraordinary circumstances brought other children to Indersdorf, for instance the young Ukrainian Alexander Pecha, called Peter in the children's center. His parents had been shot in Shitomir, Ukraine. An SS doctor named Bruhns had kept the youngster for years as a mascot, calling him Siegfried Bruhns and teaching him Nazi songs and poems. After the physician abandoned him in East Prussia in 1944, a German woman took him in. She had no idea of his real history but noticed that he often used Russian words. She discovered his name purely by accident when one day she picked up a glass of face cream and absent-mindedly read the manufacturers' name aloud: "Pecha." The boy suddenly knew, this was his family name, too. He was Alexander Pecha. His foster mother fled with him out of East Prussia over Czechoslovakia to Bavaria where she turned him over to the UNRRA.[100] Or, another example is little Claude Huet.[101] When he was nine, he lost his parents in the bombing of Rouen in May 1944. When the American troops arrived, he tagged along with them for a number of months doing odd jobs. In return "he was given shelter, food, clothing and a sympathetic ear. It was only when the soldiers were ordered to turn over such youngsters to the Military Police that the end of his migration seemed in view."[102] All of these children were cared for in Indersdorf until they could return to their home countries.

Displaced Babies

Even newborns and toddlers could be considered DPs if their mothers or both parents were foreigners: "As soon as we opened the place people brought us children from German institutions, children [of] forced laborers where the mothers were not allowed to marry and where the child was taken away from her."[103] In Indersdorf as well, a "foreign children's nursery" was set up directly behind the convent walls, and from September 1944 to May 1945, this run-down house, called "Kinderbaracke," received the babies that forced laborers were required to give up. Of 62 registered infants, 34 died from lack of care shortly after arrival.[104]

Five of these undernourished and neglected children were among the first that UNRRA Team 182 took in,[105] not unlike the Polish boy Jura Piatek, born in April 1944 in Dachau[106], who survived the notorious "Kinderbaracke" in Indersdorf. Greta Fischer describes him in October 1945 as retarded in his development, a passive child who would make only very slow progress.[107]

Some of the smallest children had been abandoned in hospitals by their mothers when they returned to their countries of origin after liberation.[108] Many had been rejected because their fathers were German or the mothers were too ashamed to return with an illegitimate child. Still other mothers left their offspring temporarily until they could ascertain what the home situation was really like.[109]

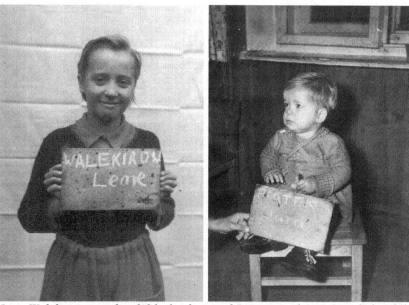

Lene Walekirow was the child of a deceased Russian and Jura Piatek the child of a Polish forced laborer. They had survived the notorious "Kinderbaracke" in Indersdorf.

It also happened that a parent was prevented from coming to collect her children, as in the case of Therese Divak, whose mother, a Soviet forced laborer, died in a Dachau hospital shortly after liberation. When an UNRRA team found the baby, she had an inflated stomach and was too weak to hold her head up.[110]

Moreover, many of the infants had odysseys behind them. A group of forced laborers' children came, for instance, from Oberglogau [Głogówek] in Silesia. In the confusion of the war's ending, the little ones had been hurriedly transported without their parents knowing about it. First they went to Ullersdorf near Dresden and from there to Buchelsdorf (Bukowa Slaska) in Upper Silesia, and then back to Ullersdorf and finally to County Kötzting (Bavaria) where they were found by an UNRRA search team.[111]

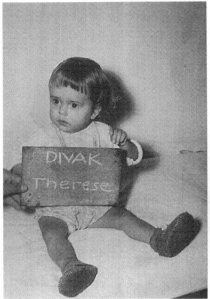

Therese Divak, child of a deceased Russian forced laborer, was found in Dachau. Daniel Mariewski (Baumann) was born in Munich. His mother was stateless, his father a German Wehrmacht officer.

If their mothers were foreigners, children from "Lebensborn" institutions also found shelter at Indersdorf.[112] Greta Fischer suspected that "another group of infants [was] apparently children of Allied National mothers and German fathers, members of the party ... to whom the women were awarded in somewhat the same manner in which they might have been given an extra ration."[113] These little ones tended to be in better physical condition than the children of forced laborers, and toward the end of the war, many of them were brought to a collection point in Steinhöring, east of Munich. "When the US Army reached Steinhöring, all archival documents had already been destroyed. Nothing was left concerning the children but index cards with brief information on first and last names, birthdates and place of birth."[114] Thus they arrived in Indersdorf with only little information about their identity. When a reporter from the *Süddeutsche Zeitung* in December 1945 saw so many displaced babies at the cloister, he wrote, "Later, when these orphans have become big boys and girls, they are certain to ask 'Where is my mother?' Then they will be told the story of the Nazis."[115] Just like the bigger ones, the youngest children found in Kloster Indersdorf a protective environment in which to feel safe until long-term arrangements could be made.

Walter Beausert (front left) was born in a "Lebensborn" house near Paris. His mother was French and his father German. 67 years later he is still searching for his roots.

Creating a Therapeutic Environment

Caregivers were confronted not only with children under three years of age who presented all the typical signs of neglect, such as "pot bellies, head-tossing, screaming in their sleep ... little interest in their surroundings, continuous mild whimpering" or "not enough energy to cry, and no smiling."[116] An eighteen-month-old girl couldn't yet sit up and her skin hung on her bones; a one-year-old was covered with scabies. Moreover, within a short time more than 100 young people of various nationalities arrived. They had suffered deprivation and humiliation of such unimaginable types and intensity that their sense of security had been profoundly shaken; often they had been through a myriad of traumatizing experiences.[117] Many hurt from the loss of family and the security of home; all hungered for individual physical and emotional attention. They had vegetated long enough as "Untermenschen" and uniformed slaves: The importance to the children of being considered individuals upon reception at the center was obvious. They were welcomed by a team member, who introduced himself, explained the center and the reception process rather than instructing the child to do this and go there. Newcomers were immediately introduced to "oldtimers" who were asked to take them in tow and show them the center.[118]

To avoid contagious diseases such as typhus, the children were first deloused with DDT,[119] examined by a doctor and cared for by a nurse; they were given clean clothes, were bathed, fed, and assigned bunks. Often in the first interview, caregivers heard about the most unimaginable cruelties that these "children" had endured, what happened to their families and friends, whom they had lost and whom they still hoped to find.

In the Children's Center's early days, employees had to manage everything at once. Greta Fischer described her team's priorities: "The first thing was to give them food, plenty of food, to give them clothing, which was difficult, and to listen to their stories."[120] Because reliable teachers and instructors were in short supply, the approximately 150 five- to sixteen-year-olds had to make due with five classes, hardly any free time activities and no supervision during the day or night.[121] Sister Dolorosa's desperate letter of September 20, 1945, sheds light on conditions in her beloved cloister: "We scrubbed the old dirt away for six whole weeks so that, except for the walls, it was really quite clean. Everyone was happy. Then the "children" arrived, boys and young men up to twenty-four years, poor people from the concentration camps but who are totally unreceptive to ideas of order and cleanliness. Everything that could possibly be scuffed and dirtied was. Indersdorf has surely never been as filthy as now. It doesn't matter how much you clean and tidy up. It makes no difference because the kids hang around inside and outside the whole day long with nothing to do and have to busy themselves with something."[122]

UNRRA social worker André Marx welcomes the Ukranian boy Alexander Pecha at the main entrance of Kloster Indersdorf.

Despite the urgency, UNRRA workers could only deal with issues one at a time. The very name UNRRA prioritized the mission: the first "R" stood for "relief" which meant alleviating immediate physical pain and taking care of basic needs. The first priority was giving new arrivals food and clothing, a hot bath, a clean bed of their own and medical attention. Only after reliable Displaced Persons and representatives of other aid organizations had been hired as caregivers and teachers, could the employees gradually focus on basic, enduring issues of the children's and young people's "rehabilitation," the second "R" in UNRRA. The idea was to give the youngsters as quickly as possible what they needed to piece together the fragments of their shattered lives and enable them to face a new future. "Relief" and "Rehabilitation" worked in tandem and together described the therapeutic milieu designed to give the young survivors a chance to return to normal life.

Twenty-five-year old Mordecai Topel pouring tea. This Jewish survivor of Flossenbürg concentration camp was among the oldest who were cared for in the children's center.

Satisfying the need for food

The youngsters knew only too well that in the concentration camp a piece of bread had often made the difference between life and death.[123] Now they faced the opposite situation: food that they had long had to do without or, in some cases, had never seen before, appeared on the table: pancakes, eggs, orange juice, ham, cookies and white bread. Bread was the most important and desired food.

It was freshly baked every day and delivered in large quantities by local bakeries. The caregivers understood that the young people continued to feel as though they were starving and would want twice as much as their peers. Generous portions were expected to fulfill a therapeutic aim: "It was the team's belief that to be liberal with food would help the youngsters to get over their craving to have and to hold bread and the fear that there would not be another meal."[124] The survivors had to be given time to overcome their fierce longing for nourishment, and normal portions would have frustrated them. Some, however, after years of privation, required a special diet in which quantities increased gradually. In this regard, Joseph Conrady, officer in the mess hall, could only improvise since a cook trained as a dietician, who had indeed been requested from higher-ranking authorities, never arrived.

Cooking took place in three large kitchens; in the dining room meals were served in shifts – due to lack of space and inadequate amounts of silver- and dinnerware. From the start, the daily ration contained around 2,000 calories per person, although the bigger children who needed to catch up received more while the smaller children got less. Breakfast consisted of oatmeal, milk, bread and butter; at noon there were meat, vegetables, and some sort of carbohydrate plus bread, butter and fruit; in the evening soup, potatoes, vegetables, cheese and "other proteins." At 10 a.m. and at 3 p.m. snacks were served: bread, jam, milk and cocoa.[125] Occasionally, the team also prepared special treats for the kids – a chunk of chocolate, a birthday cake, or a particular ethnic food they remembered. [126]

Not infrequently, the teens would eat double the normal portion so that the less athletic among them gained a considerable amount of weight, as Genia Edlermann noted, blaming her high butter consumption for her rapid growth in size.[127]

Greta Fischer helps a group of toddlers at mealtime.

The UNRRA team was astonished at how long the children's excessive desire for food continued even after their bodies had visibly recovered. Eating therefore seemed to be a psychological compensation for suffering. After talking to the center's physician, the staff decided that the children would continue to receive more than normal rations. The regular mealtimes and generous portions were thus intended to strengthen the victims' confidence that the times of scarcity were truly over. They were supposed to learn to trust in daily routines, to leave behind the extreme psychological trials they had gone through, and to return to a kind of normality. As Greta Fischer confirmed: "The amounts of food consumed were enormous. Even when they recovered their health, the desire for food continued. In discussing the problem with the center's physician, it became clear to the staff that until other psychological satisfactions could be achieved for these children — a slow process even under different and more appropriate circumstances — the children should be served more than the normal ration allocated." She went on: "One of the older boys explained that taking bread from the dining room was almost an unconscious act. Having had so little for so long, never knowing from where and when the next bit of food would come from — it was almost impossible to believe that there would always be a next meal and a next one."[128] They harbored a deep-seated fear that what they received could easily be torn away. As Fischer noted, "… when I saw some of these youngsters 30 - 40 years later, some of them [still] took a little piece of bread under their pillow in order to make sure there would be a next meal. The fear never disappears."[129]

In the camps or the woods, youngsters had not only gone hungry; they had also suffered horrible hygienic conditions. They were no longer accustomed to sitting down to eat and using tableware. Often in the blink of an eye they would snatch their food and throw it down their throats, or else hide it in their pockets. If survivors were to be helped to enjoy a sort of normal life, it was clear that table manners would have to be part of the training.[130]

Team members discussed among themselves "what kind of life the children would have led" had their parents lived and oriented themselves according to the norms of typical, middle-class customs that many of the children had surely experienced before.[131] The UNRRA staff wanted to create a relaxed atmosphere without becoming too *laissez-faire*. In family-like groups with one grown-up at the table as a model, the youngsters would be reintroduced to table manners: "The service in the dining-room is simple but intended to maintain neatness and an informal atmosphere of order. When two courses are served, different plates are used. Serving dishes and silver are used. The children are served in family style, eight to ten sitting at one table."[132] Greta Fischer noted that both the more cultivated style of eating and the family-like groups increased the young survivors' self-respect and level of comfort. The Allies' team of psychologists also recommended family-like groups, even if the youngsters were staying at Indersdorf only for a very short time. All should enjoy at least briefly a kind of "secure family life" and be cared for by "confident, friendly grown-ups."[133]

Eating together in family-like groups with one grown-up at the table, setting a pattern.

Struggling to restore health

Years of starvation meant that many youngsters were small for their age, had problems with their teeth or eyes, were "infested with scabies, impetigo, and similar filth diseases. These, of course, contributed to the discomfort of the children, making them fretful during sleep as well as when awake."[134] UNRRA staff understood the relationship between body and mind and knew that many of these problems were caused by "separation, neglect, rejection, oppression and physical abuse."[135]

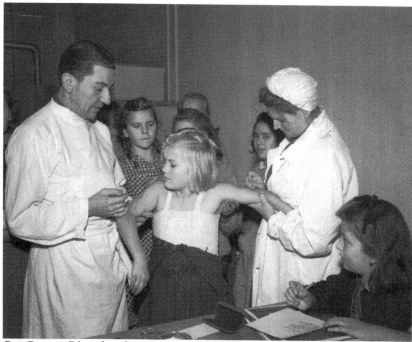

Dr. Gaston Gérard and a nurse inoculate the children against contagious diseases.

Babies' health was often especially alarming: first-aid was required immediately if the most endangered were to survive. Greta Fischer offers examples: "One child of 19 months, unable to sit up unsupported; another of 21 months who appeared to be dying of ennui. At first both children were almost entirely unresponsive to external stimuli."[136] From the start, these children had to be given intensive care. Their food was enriched with vitamins; they were offered "sunlight therapy," that is, whenever the sun was shining, they were cared for outdoors in the convent's large garden. "They were given not only physical care, but also psychological attention — fondled in an attempt to compensate for mother love."[137] Most reacted positively to this special treatment. After only a couple of months, progress was visible. Even these two "recovered and, although they lagged behind their own age group, at about 24 months they could stand with support and shortly thereafter, they walked unaided. Both children [at first] were relatively shy in group activity, but they participated with interest as they improved physically."[138]

Every new arrival in Indersdorf would undergo a thorough examination by a doctor and a nurse, was deloused, weighed and inoculated against typhus, small pox, typhoid and diphtheria.[139] But many of the youngsters resisted. Whether distrustful or merely ignorant, they had to be restrained. Jakob Hecht from Romania, for instance, then 15, recalls today as Jack Hecht, with a wry smile, how in Kloster Indersdorf he had to be held down on the ground by other boys in order to receive the shot given for his own good.

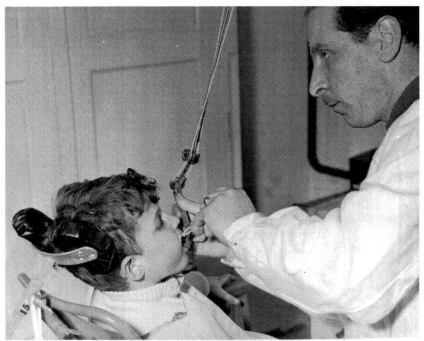

Regular check-ups: Polish-Jewish dentist Dr. Josef Unger, himself a survivor of Dachau Concentration Camp, with patient Alexander Pecha.

Eugenius Kamer, for example, a Jewish survivor of Mauthausen concentration camp, soon started to cough heavily and eventually became very ill. Because of widespread tuberculosis, nearly all children were x-rayed as a preventive measure; and if positive, a child like Eugenius Kamer was sent immediately to the DP tuberculosis clinic in Gauting. In the Children's Center an on-site dental clinic was soon set up where Unger worked, Dr. Josef Unger, a newly liberated dentist who had been captive in Dachau concentration camp before.[140] From time to time, special clinics in Munich treated the young survivors, especially when they needed eye examinations.[141]

To check up on the health of each individual child, all those under five were weighed twice a week and older ones once a week. Part of the health regime included instruction in bodily hygiene; the children were also expected to brush their teeth. Most, fortunately, found bathing a pleasure, something many had longed for during the war.[142]

To prevent the outbreak of infectious diseases, some children had to be separated from the rest and placed under quarantine. In April 1946 a dramatic situation arose when two new arrivals were not recognized as carrying TB and diphtheria. While fortunately no one fell ill despite exposure to active tuberculosis, two German maids and seven small children caught diphtheria, and two of the little ones died in a Munich hospital.[143] In the convent, an immediate suspension of new arrivals went into effect, and all residents were put under a fortnight's quarantine.[144] During this time, lessons, meals, and sleep — in fact, all activities — took place in the bedrooms. "During the quarantine we were able to collect some radios which we put in the various isolation rooms. The girls made play suits and other clothing out of material we had in the warehouse. The boys did various kinds of handicraft work. We provided all the children with as many kinds of games as we had on hand and with reading material given to us by voluntary agencies and the UNRRA."[145] Once the two-week period was over and all suspicious incidents had been medically treated, the quarantine was lifted on May 26, and things went back to normal.[146]

From the start the health of premature twins Josef and Alfred Lamzek kept the staff on edge. Upon arrival at the Children's Center, both were extremely underweight for their three months. "Despite special nourishment, blood transfusions and careful observation,"[147] for several weeks, the staff was unable to save them.[148] While the health of most children and young people in Kloster Indersdorf clearly improved between July 1945 and July 1946, six small children died from various illnesses.[149]

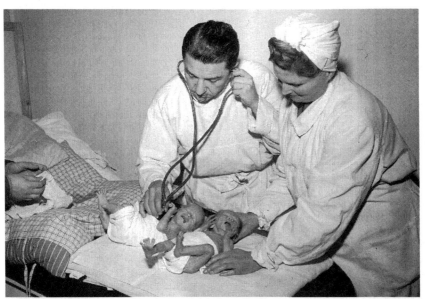

Dr. Gaston Gérard and a nurse struggle to save the lives of twins Josef and Alfred Lamzek (1945)

Individual clothing styles and self-esteem

Concentration camp survivors needed to get rid of their filthy, lice-infested uniforms as quickly as possible to enable them to feel like girls and boys again and no longer like genderless slave laborers. The girls longed to wear skirts and dresses again. The boys treasured watches, belts or a pair of leather boots as significant status symbols.[150] The clothing contributed to replenishing self-esteem.

For instance, as the group of survivors from the Flossenbürg camp arrived at the end of August 1945, they took special pleasure in receiving right away snow-white pullovers in the appropriate sizes. At least fifty white knitted sweaters were on hand, and thus the youngsters wearing them could be identified as newly arrived. Later this knitwear came to signal those who had been there longer.

Marion E. Hutton helps Polish girl Zofia Karpuk to find the right clothes (November 1945).

The UNRRA team considered it important for rehabilitation as well as therapy to allow survivors to choose for themselves the style, color and pattern of their clothes in order to feel like individuals and not just a number among numbers, a degradation they had suffered for years in the camps. They were also encouraged to show their own taste and to make their own decisions, even if these concerned "only" their attire. "Clothing was simple but fitted to size and whenever possible children were encouraged to choose colors and patterns." Greta Fischer discovered that appropriate clothing could indeed influence a young person for the better: "The entire personality of a child seemed to change when the old, dirty, misshapen garments were replaced by clean, well-fitting and non-institutional clothes. ... Apart from the feeling of well-being, it contributed to the re-establishment of a sense of personal worth, dignity, decency and warmth."[151]

A journalist from the *Neue Zeitung* who visited the Children's Center in October 1945 compared the store rooms to a miniature department store: "Here you find everything from diapers, rubber sheets and baby clothes for the littlest ones to dirndls, pullovers, belts and clogs for girls, and suits, winter coats and boots for boys." The goods came in part from Wehrmacht [German Army] inventories, but mostly from the U.K. and the USA. "A box of American blouses made of camouflage is still full. None of the kids wants to wear them because they are too much like the SS apparel, and for that reason they don't like them."[152]

These little ones are wearing clothes made of bedding and material from Nazi flags.

To procure cloth, team members often traveled to nearby Dachau where Greta Fischer visited the newly liberated concentration camp: "There was Dachau which stood for the death of so many people. And there I was looking for material to clothe children who would be growing up for what? I didn't know at the time."[153] In a building requisitioned by the US Army on the former Dachau SS compound, she hit pay dirt: "I saw huge roles of red material which was the flag material; the Nazi flag was red, and there were huge roles of blue and white cotton material, which the Germans used for their bedding." The workshop in the center made the material into clothing for infants and toddlers. "We designed a red heart and blue and white pants, or vice versa, we had red pants and a blue and white checked heart and the children looked adorable, you know, they looked like little French sailors."[154] In this way the staff was able at least to do something useful with Nazi surplus.

In addition to new clothing, used clothes had to be altered and improved; old army blankets and such material were transformed into outfits. Older girls and boys interested in a tailor's apprenticeship were encouraged to sew their own garments.

British storeroom manager Harry C. Parker is fitting Alexander Pecha with new shoes.

After years of hard work wearing wooden shoes or grossly ill-fitting footwear, all survivors and also the children found leather shoes to be a treasure. For instance, when in the Föhrenwald camp Polish but not Jewish inmates got new shoes, a revolt broke out.[155] It is unknown whether any similar incident occurred in Indersdorf. Nonetheless, here too – despite efficient distribution – staff found articles of clothing lacking, such as socks, girls' stockings or pajamas.[156] And temporary scarcity occurred if neither the UNRRA, the US Army nor the immediate environment could supply a wardrobe with garments that were difficult to make oneself.

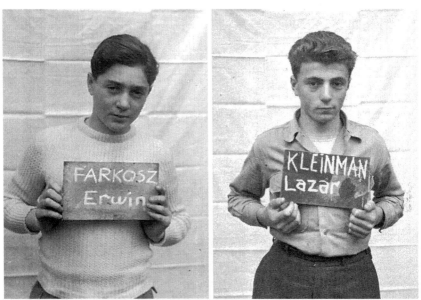

Erwin Farkas, his brother Zoltán and Lazar (Leslie) Kleinmann had supported each other on a death march.

Survivors cling to each other

Lazar Kleinmann, who came to Indersdorf in August 1945, having lost his entire family — parents and seven siblings — "was very restless until he could be assured that his two best friends who had lived through many experiences with him could also be admitted to the center."[157] Only after arrival of the brothers Zoltán and Erwin Farkas, whom he had known from his hometown in the Carpathian Mountains, was he able to calm down. Youths who had lived through Nazi atrocities together vehemently refused to be separated from those they had been with, having formed surrogate family groups. They offered each other mutual support and security, and felt as though the others also understood their traumatizing experience because only those who had gone through it could really know what Auschwitz or Flossenbürg meant. Therefore, it was important to take the children's wishes into account: "Next to the desire to find relatives, was the need for remaining with friends, especially those who had experienced similar hardships in the same ghettos or camps. Child after child asked to be allowed to sleep in the same room with his friends ..."[158]

In the dormitory, youngsters could choose to be with their friends and to decorate the room according to their preferences.

Compared to the considerable amount of space in the large DP camps Föhrenwald or Landsberg,[159] conditions in Indersdorf could be considered luxurious. The building might easily have housed 500 people,[160] but because rooms were used for lessons and recreation, twelve to 25 girls and boys shared sleeping quarters. Each was assigned a single bed and clean sheets even after the number of youths admitted in the spring of 1946 rose.[161] The children were permitted to choose their roommates "with no restriction for age, sex, or nationality, only limited by the number of beds available in a given room and the separation of boys and girls of adolescent years. This latter restriction was not expressed;

it was tacitly assumed."[162] Criteria of choice also comprised nationality, language and religious belief: "Since most of the children chose their roommates from among their compatriots, the walls of the various rooms were soon decorated with national emblems and other reminders of home."[163] The Polish Gentile boys hung a large red and white national flag on the wall and the Polish Jewish boys preferred pictures of their Zionist idols. Because the UNRRA team admired the sense of cohesiveness among the children of the same age-group, staff encouraged each room to choose a leader and an assistant leader. These delegates in turn joined others, thirty-five in all, to form a "House Council" or "Children's Council" that met once a week with UNRRA representatives and grown-up DPs for practice in self-governance. The room heads were responsible for tidiness and order as well as conveying their roommates' desires to the UNRRA welfare officers.[164] Often what they wanted was leisure activities.[165]

Babies need individual care

In fall 1945 the *UNRRA Review of the month* must have had especially the babies of forced laborers in mind when it reported from Indersdorf, "Of the total population nearly one-fifth are under two years of age and this group have in some ways suffered most of all. The babies of six months and under were at least half the normal size and bore acute signs of under-nourishment. All of these infants have had their growth arrested by at least six months, in many cases even longer. Aid for these infants was urgent if they were to survive. Vitamin feeding was instituted and sunray treatment given. Within three days the infants could be induced to smile and the rashes on their faces were disappearing. Now, apart from their pathetic thinness of their limbs, which will take many months to fill out, the babies of Kloster Indersdorf are happy and healthy."[166]

Greta Fischer knew that intense devotion is required most urgently during the first years of life to ensure a healthy development of basic trust. Individual care for the smallest, to overcome developmental deficiencies and promote well-rounded growth, should therefore take place in small groups; continuous care by a single person was essential to "compensate for the lack of mother love" and allow the children with obvious developmental delays to catch up and become "emotionally alert."[167] Given the egregious lack of personnel, groups were formed with 12 to 15 boys and girls divided according to stage of development and need for attention and care: infants were in one group; then came those who could already sit up by themselves, had begun to feed themselves, crawl and stand. In the third group that later became a sort of pre-nursery school class were those who could eat independently, almost dress themselves, go to the toilet and walk. For each group, Greta Fischer trained two or three DP assistants, teaching them childcare and therapy; each was accompanied by one of the nuns. They were expected to cultivate a personal relationship to the little ones who, by virtue of regular care and immediate response to their needs, would recuperate a measure of security and trust.

Sister Adelgunde Flierl with two-year-olds.

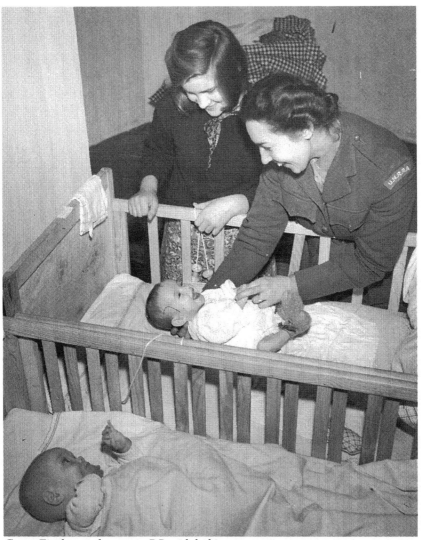
Greta Fischer and a young DP with babies.

After only a few weeks, the smallest ones grew calmer, once they noticed how regularly and responsibly the same person took care of them, like, for instance, little Jean Pierre.[168] In January, 1946, Greta Fischer observed that at "20 months [he] had such absence of response that it was feared he was mentally defective, possibly autistic. ... After continued special care, however, he suddenly became more alert, his eyes began to focus with interest on the persons around him and the play material which was strung across his crib. He began to sit up, and today he is one of the most active members of the nursery school group, running gleefully after the children and just beginning to talk."[169] Fischer estimated that the youngest ones needed at least a year to make up for the starvation and neglect they had undergone. Plenty of patience, attention and personal care were needed before the first smile lit up a little face,[170] a certain and wonderful sign of healing for body and soul. As this dedicated social worker remarked, "Seeing the first spontaneous smile on a child's face or his reaching out for contact are moments never to be forgotten."[171]

Also many boys loved to care for the babies.

The UNRRA team and the Sisters of Mercy rejoiced at most of the small children's rapid progress and saw their own priorities confirmed. Even the UNRRA investigation unit, in November 1945, was convinced not to send babies to another camp because they were impressed at how the nuns were giving them special, individual attention. "It is suggested that the group of infants remain in the center rather than be moved to Wartenberg, particularly in view of the capability of the sisters who are giving direct care."[172]

Girls from Upper Silesia play godparents to the babies (from left: Martha Cierpiol, Wanda Bunzol, unidentified).

The considerable span in resident children's ages at Indersdorf had one advantage: the older ones could help care for the younger. Many did this of their own free will, thereby creating a family-like atmosphere that was good not only for the babies, but for their caregivers as well. The UNRRA staff also found this arrangement "most salubrious"[173] for the youths who played godparents to smaller children, feeding them, bathing them and playing with them. The task kept the teens from senseless boredom and afforded personal fulfillment. And many of the young Holocaust survivors mourned not only for younger siblings and cousins, but also in a sense for their infant selves: by caring for the little ones, memories awoke in them of their own childhoods before persecution and, for both girls and boys, brought back to life a tender, softer side they had not been permitted to express in the camps.[174] For that reason the UNRRA staff in Indersdorf strove to contradict their superiors, who wanted separate children's centers for various age groups;[175] and they emphasized in their reports the recurrent opportunities in having the little ones, older children and teens living together.

Easing the young people's hearts

The newly arrived wanted above all else to talk about their unspeakable experiences. For days on end, entire groups followed and besieged the counselors on their daily rounds in order to tell them what they had suffered during the war years. Their one desire was to release all their bottled-up self-expression, and by a flood of talk to somehow cope with their memories of fear and horror. They forced UNRRA staff to sit down and listen, attentively and patiently. Of the first 192 residents, fully 125 needed immediate psychological counseling. Social workers suddenly found themselves confronted by teenagers who had been rounded up at gunpoint in Polish villages, transported and forced into slave labor in Germany, who had drudged in concentration camps and experienced up close the murder of their loved ones. Imagine the condition of people like, for instance, Sacher Israeler, who as a ten-year-old following a German "Aktion" in the ghetto found his mother and sister in the street, shot dead, and had to watch as his father, with a bullet in his jaw, bled to death?! Some of the Jewish boys had delivered corpses to the crematoria; they had to cut down those that had been hanged.

These Jewish survivors from Poland today live as Jack Bulwa in California and Zwi Weinstock in Israel.

Jakob Bulwa was only 13 and Hermann Weinstock a tender seven when the persecution began for them. UNRRA volunteers had not been prepared to face survivors with such deep psychological wounds, who told what they knew in voices sometimes highly pitched and tense, sometimes monotone, but always about unimaginable cruelties. The Sisters of Mercy felt a special empathy for one seventeen-year-old Polish Jewish boy whom they describe as "extraordinarily gentle and intelligent." When in the concentration camp, he witnessed "his parents, in particular his mother being incinerated, he lost his sanity. He was often a pitiable sight when this kind young man spent half the night sitting on the stone staircase of the convent weeping and whimpering like a little child."[176] The youngsters often had a whole trail of traumatic experiences behind them although the violent separation from their murdered parents had left the deepest wounds. Even the Allies' psychological experts encouraged recognition of this phenomenon: "The need to be loved and valued ... and to possess affectionate relationships with friends, is perhaps the deepest of all human needs. For this reason deprivation of affectionate ties with others is perhaps the most damaging emotional hurt which a human being can receive."[177]

UNRRA Team 182 also took care of a few youngsters who had already lost their parents in their homelands and had therefore been raised by foster- or grandparents. Most of these children, in Greta Fischer's views, did not suffer such severe trauma as those already older children whose parents were suddenly and brutally ripped away.

Jewish youth showed their Auschwitz tattoos and had an intense need to reveal what they had gone through in the camps. "When the children first arrived at Kloster Indersdorf, they talked and talked and talked about their experiences in the concentration camps and as slave laborers. Horror stories were intermingled with ordinary events with little demonstration of emotion."[178] The UNRRA staff was at first overwhelmed by such unimaginable tortures as they "broke out" of these disturbed youth. Standing before them were teenagers who clearly wanted them to understand what had happened. The young people wanted their statements to be believed so that they, too, could comprehend the incomprehensible. Their testimonies were not only shocking; they sometimes even had the effect of traumatizing the attentive, sensitive listeners in turn.

Most volunteers, not only the UNRRA staff in the DP camps, were overwhelmed when confronted by tales of such brutality. "Even Jewish representatives from abroad thought that repression of memories was necessary for rehabilitation, but this ran counter to the survivors' instinctive need to retell and rework the past."[179] Like adult survivors these youngsters were constantly preoccupied with their experiences under the Nazis – "gruesome recapitulation of concentration camp incidents combined with vows of undying loyalty to these memories and hopes for vengeance."[180]

In the Indersdorf center the emotional challenge was significant, to listen to all the distraught young people and deliver oneself up to their descriptions. Greta Fischer admits that at times, the staff wept with their charges. "But you don't help children when you cry with them. We had to be brave ourselves."[181] The caregivers heard burdensome tales that "human reason simply refuse[d] to accept." Often the staff would talk among themselves about having become "somehow numbed." "We didn't permit ourselves really to feel in some ways because it was too terrible. We wouldn't have been able to do our jobs."[182] With hindsight, Greta Fischer saw the extreme amount of work that kept staff so busy as a good thing: "Every minute of the day we were asked to be there for somebody. Was it for the babies? Was it for the big children? Was it to look for material? Was it to look for food? Was it to fill out a requisition — every minute of the day? And we did pretty normal, I think."[183]

Marion E. Hutton and her colleague listen to a survivor telling his horrendous history.

Given her experience with Freudian theories of childhood trauma therapy, Greta Fischer felt that young survivors needed grown-ups to heed them, understand them and show sympathy with them. "We listened to their stories day and night. It had to come out. And sometimes it would take us hours to sit with them. You could not interrupt."[184] Although caregivers found themselves confronted by absolute horror, they learned to withstand it.

Nonetheless, when some of the children told their stories "not just once, but many times, [they] provoked another reaction, which sometimes we were a little worried about. It became very automatic. The first story came out with a lot of feeling. [But] you can't have feelings [like those] over and over again. ... They would talk about those terrible things like our children ... talk about a fairy tale. And sometimes that bothered us. But they had to tell their stories ... many times."[185] Erwin Farkas, himself one of these child survivors and today a psychologist, found benefit in repeated narrations, above all because it helped to gain distance from the experience. "Then it became a story, a story you could take or push aside – [and] somehow deal with it."[186] It became a tale with which you could live – or had to live. But he went on, "I know that I can't stand imagining how my mother is killed in the gas chamber — because I can't deal with it! I look only at recollections I can deal with."[187]

On October 31, 1945 these boys could fly to England and start a new life.

Nonetheless, "even some of the older children seem[ed] to learn to smile at the center. Manfred, age 14, is a German Jew (...) of fairly well-to-do parents who lived in Stettin. The family was deported to Poland in 1940. The father is known to be dead, the mother probably so. When one of the UNRRA team extended her hand to greet him, he shrank [but] then timidly took it. It was several days before he relaxed sufficiently to be able to join in the activities of the center. He was given as much special attention as circumstances permitted and has become one of the most popular of the youngsters. He laughs now although in moments of repose one still sees the lines of strain on his face."[188]

The UNRRA team set out from the premise that it would indeed be wholesome to remember. Those few girls and boys who did not talk about their experiences would be invited with caution to open up. Yet there were children who could not talk at all, who really had repressed their memories. "I think it was a psychological reaction. You really blocked out your stories. We had a couple of youngsters who were completely blank and we tried to help them to remember, but it took a very long time for some of those children to remember."[189]

Greta Fischer thinks that one reason the Indersdorf center had no suicides was due to the residents being encouraged to remember positive experiences as well.[190] In discussion, social workers asked survivors not only about what happened in the camps, but also what happened before. Inner strength appears to have been generated by questions relating to childhood and life with their parents at home. If a child's face would brighten up when talking about family background, this was a sure sign of personal resources. Most of the youngsters did indeed remember their childhoods and family lives. Even if those lives weren't ideal, they were always inexpressibly better than what came afterward in the camps. Fourteen-year-old Miklos Roth could still feel how it was to sit on his mother's lap while she sang him a song. He still knew the taste of the goose liver that she had always so expertly prepared, and above all the sense of security he had had there. Today Imre Hitter thinks that the camps left him bereft of everything except his "good upbringing and knowledge of the meaning the name of Hitter once carried in his Hungarian hometown."[191] Greta Fischer felt that those young survivors who had enjoyed a happy childhood were "stronger." Her talks with center residents convinced her of the importance of the earliest years for laying a foundation solid enough to support later burdens and challenges – despite excessive trauma. In the camps these children drew on early emotional connections; these memories formed protective scaffolding for life. By looking back on satisfying moments from childhood before internment and drawing on earlier experience, they were able to summon inner strength and find the courage to live once more.

The UNRRA team's aim was to give each child a feeling of security along with an understanding that he or she was desired and loved.[192] Yet survivors' distrust often ran deep. For instance, JOINT[193] social worker Miriam Warburg encountered a situation in which the Jewish children in the Föhrenwald DP camp accused their counselors of theft when the latter replaced non-kosher meat in the JOINT care packages with cans of condensed milk.[194] Naturally, children's attitudes toward their caregivers in Indersdorf varied with the counselors' own abilities and empathy. Not every staff member was able to keep in mind the details of each child's fate or to behave with constant sensitivity and understanding when confronted with various horrors.[195] Toward the end of 1945 an UNRRA inspection team observed, "Individual security now seems to lie largely with Mr. Marx and Miss Fischer. This is understandable in view of their capabilities and functions, but they cannot spread themselves [so far as] to meet the emotional needs of the whole group."[196] Thus it soon became clear how much better it was to assign each youngster on arrival one specific counselor, someone to offer all-around care, listen, become acquainted with his or her physical and psychological problems, understand how best to handle reintegration, follow progress in school and in general guide the child's all-around development. Each youngster needed to feel that one social worker was personally responsible and that the two of them would make plans together, not that random assignment would allot their advisors. Trust, if any, the young survivors could grant only to individual caregivers. The UNRRA inspection report therefore recommended that the bedrooms of house mothers and fathers be near their charges' dormitories "to add to the feeling of belonging and … make supervision easier and less formal."[197] Sadly, a dearth of reliable DPs made this recommendation difficult to implement. One document in particular shows just how keen a group of youth were to remain close to a trusted staff member. When Helen Steiger was transferred from the Social Work department at Indersdorf to another DP camp, 21 Jewish survivors found her loss oppressive. They therefore petitioned UNRRA Headquarters:[198]

> To
> U.N.R.R.A. Hqu.
>
> From D.P.Children Center.Team 182
> Indersdorf.
>
> Petition.
>
> We, the undersigned children of the D.P. ChildrennCenter are addressing to You this request.
> Several days ago, Miss Steiger, who acted as Welfare Officer here had been transferred to another center. Miss Steiger had been here with us since our arrival to this Center and was regarded by us, orphan children as our mother. Miss Steigerś transfer is equivalent to the loss of a mother for us, who do not have parents. We hope that our first request which has been expressed from the very depth of our hearts will meet Your attention and will be taken into handling with a good resulted, and Miss Steiger will come to us back.
>
> The Children
> [signatures]
>
> 3 Children interviewed, when they personally presented this request. Informal interpretation by their feelings about Miss Steiger comes. He said to the Director. Explained no change could be made in this S'd temporary assignment (is Army Forcing Team. Informed

To give weight to their appeal, three group representatives appeared in person to present the petition to one of the branch offices of UNRRA. They achieved their aim of bringing her back to Indersdorf.

In general, it could be observed in the DP camps that the young people rebelled against "any form of top-down organization behind which they suspected the old, despised coercion that they had just lived through."[199] In the Indersdorf Children's Center, survivors demonstrated a creative form of revolt. "For example, boys who were on the playground when the bell rang for dinner would line up in rigid formation, act like automatons and goose-step in military order into the hall."[200]

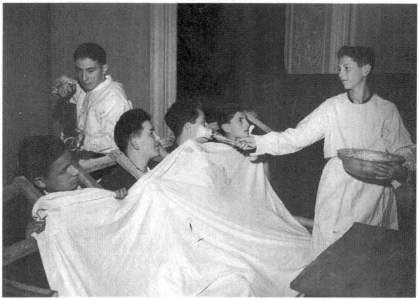

Survivors play-act their concentration camp experiences. Salek Benedikt (in the back with "disinfection spray") recalls that this scene was to be performed for General Eisenhower.

The youths reacted with anger whenever anything reminded them of Nazi rule. For instance, UNRRA staff, who felt obliged to take attendance because unauthorized persons would repeatedly slip in to find shelter, provoked the children into staging a kind of demonstration: "Spontaneous dramatic activity took place on many occasions. For example, when one evening the staff decided to have a roll call in the children's bedrooms, they were met by a line-up of the boys dressed in their old concentration camp uniforms. A 'storm trooper' at the end of the line shouted each name and if not answered promptly, struck or 'shot' the culprit. The boys considered this good fun, but in a subtle (or maybe not so subtle) way they wanted to tell the UNRRA team that they wished to be treated as individuals and trusted."[201]

At first the staff was startled and shocked, but once the young people's motives were understood, such dramatic activity was actually promoted as a way to gain clarity into prior terrible events and to see them with new eyes from various vantage points.

Nearly all spontaneous games the youngsters enjoyed contained at first scenes from the concentration camps, sometimes presented with dry humor. "The children are amazingly talented and it seemed quite remarkable that after years of hardship and repression they could express themselves creatively. They frequently drew on their experiences of the past, and the satires of concentration camp life which would have been horrible to an average audience were received with enthusiastic glee."[202] While the young audience felt its own experiences mirrored and understood, caregivers noticed the therapeutic effect: "The other thing was, we used a lot of theatre to unburden them, drama. For instance, some of the boys would put their heads in a step ladder ... so that they couldn't move their heads and then others would do all kinds of cruelties to them in order to play out the cruelties they had experienced on themselves. That was a kind of group therapy. A lot of things came out in that. It was important. We tried everything to unburden them."[203]

The UNRRA staff saw that, as the victims themselves discovered, it was not repression of the horrors recently gone through but the reverse, a head-on confrontation with them that constituted the best route to healing. Therefore they promoted this early form of "psychodrama."

And little by little, the plays in Indersdorf grew more lighthearted. "The use of such material for spontaneous productions has lessened as time has passed and other more pleasant experiences are being had."[204] Gradually religious and national holidays, particularly Chanukah, Christmas, and New Year's, "became the focus of the plays."[205] Bernat Nasch, born into an Orthodox family, remembers how, on September 16, 1945, together with other

Jewish boys, he celebrated Yom Kippur, the Day of Atonement, the highest holy day, in the dining hall by refusing food. The group had decided to return to religious obligations and therefore fasted.[206]

Greta Fischer (left) with her colleague André Marx (2nd from left) at a Passover Seder in the pub "Unterbräu" in Dachau, 1946.

The first holidays after liberation — whether Rosh Hashanah, Yom Kippur, Chanukah or even Christmas or the Russian New Year — , were all celebrated in the International Children's Center Kloster Indersdorf with great intensity and "all generated a strong feeling of happiness and ecstasy, so that it is almost impossible to describe them adequately."[207] To have found herself in the spring of 1946 celebrating Pesach in Dachau of all places was for Greta Fischer a particularly moving personal experience. Jewish survivors commemorated not only the liberation of their people from Egyptian slavery, but also the millions murdered in the Shoah.

Identifying the Children

At times the Children's Center housed more than twenty different nationalities. In January 1946 Greta Fischer noted: "At the present time the majority of the children are Polish. There is a small Jewish group, chiefly of Polish origin but including some from other Eastern European countries, the Baltic countries, and a few German and Austrian Jews. Western Europeans are in the minority and are found chiefly among the younger children.

Greta Fischer is looking through the Karpuks' suitcase in hopes of finding some clue to surviving relatives. Both children lived and worked with their mother, a Polish forced laborer, on a farm in Urfar near Malching in Lower Bavaria. In February 1945 their mother died of blood poisoning. The last sign of life from their father was a letter sent at Easter 1944.

There has been a substantial group of Yugoslav children, most of whom have been repatriated."[208] The UNRRA staff spent a major portion of its time looking for parents and relations. To succeed, immediately on arrival at Kloster Indersdorf a comprehensive report on each child had to be prepared, which would then be forwarded to the Central Tracing Office in Frankfurt. The UNRRA Tracing Bureaus collected documents and other papers from children in order to find relatives in countries of origin. The central German UNRRA agency called on foreign governments to report their losses or to send representatives who could help to search for children and identify their nationalities. The UNRRA demonstrated that "international cooperation could work efficiently and effectively."[209] So-called "tracing teams" searched for the missing in German institutions and private households. They used school registrations, identification papers, ration cards, or notices seeking missing children who had been adopted by German families.[210] "Many a child was found only thanks to the initiative and intuition of a dogged worker in an UNRRA uniform."[211]

It was generally hard to identify the children, but it was most difficult to find out who the youngest were because often at the end of the war, Nazis in charge of "Kinderbaracken" or "Lebensborn" houses destroyed birth certificates and other records. "This was especially true in those instances when children had been brought to the center from German institutions that had been set up during the Nazi regime for children of slave laborers and those whose fathers had been Nazi officials."[212] Therefore a child's age sometimes had to be guessed and an approximate birthdate assigned. In case family members were searching for children, all the clothing of new arrivals had to be carefully stored. These garments might offer valuable clues to establishing a child's identity because names often helped only partially or not at all. "When for instance Barbara, about two years old, was admitted to the center, the record that accompanied her gave only a surname that seemed of Eastern European derivation, first name and birthdate unknown. She was apparently given the name Barbara at the transient camp from which she had come. Her parents' names were unknown."[213]

Intense investigation was needed to arrive at a baby's true identity. If at first no information at all was found, the child had to be given a provisional name that somehow appeared plausible.

Sofie Rybki was given both her first and last names by Zofia Karpuk.

Polish orphan Zofia Karpuk[214] told the story of one such name-giving. The ten-year-old was glad to go help take care of the infants. One baby in particular moved her so much that she was permitted to hold it. The little one had been found in Schärding, Austria, but there was no documentation of her identity. Zofia Karpuk remembers that she had given this child the nickname "little fish," in Polish "rybki," when she spotted it lying flat on its tummy in the crib. Another time when she had the baby in her arms, an UNRRA staff member asked the young assistant, "What's your name?" When she answered, "Zofia," the uniformed woman said off the cuff, the baby will be called "Sofia," too. That's how Zofia Karpuk gave Sofie Rybki both her last and first names.[215]

Soon the staff realized how difficult, if not impossible, it was to write up detailed reports on the children's identities the moment they showed up, so instead, to lose no time, they proceeded immediately to report each child's arrival and what information they had to the UNRRA Tracing Bureau. Later, more information could be added or corrections made. When, for example, Sinaida

Grussmann arrived at the Children's Center on August 30, 1945, the UNRRA team welcomed a girl who was obviously very shy with strangers. As she only reluctantly spoke a few words of Romanian and Lithuanian the social workers guessed that she was from one of these countries. The girl was only 1.21 m tall and so they assumed her birth year could be 1937. During the following months Sinaida developed a relationship of trust with Tabea Klara Langyte, a young Latvian DP teacher, and more information about her background could be revealed.[216] The staff was very surprised to find that it was not easy to get information on age, religious belief or nationality from even the older children and adolescents. This may have been due to various factors.

Sinaida Grussmann's nationality, age and religion could only be guessed. Hidrun de Maere was born at a "Lebensborn" house near Wegimont, Belgium. More details were lacking.

Jewish survivors like Abram Warszaw and Martin Hecht may have been so traumatized that they had completely forgotten their birthdays.[217] Other young people who wanted to go to England knew that they had to claim to be under 16.

Fourteen-year-old Wasil from Chernigo was orphaned and grew up without having attended school, had never known his parents' names and had not learned to distinguish between Roman Catholic and Russian Orthodox. "But he remembered well what had happened to him from the time he was taken into Germany with a group of other children in the summer of 1943."[218]

The distinction between ethnicity and nationality also caused problems. Alexander Orloff, for instance, came from Kiev in the Ukraine. When interpreter George Sedgin asked him about his nationality, he first said Ukrainian but added after a while that he was Russian. George Sedgin observed, "This undecidedness has apparently been in the youngster's mind since the time of the German aggression in Russia, when Germans intended to establish an independent Ukrainian state and the Ukrainians were supposed to be treated better than the Russians."[219] In such cases, an important clue was provided by which language the child spoke accent-free.[220]

Most had learned how advantageous, if not life-saving, it could be to alter information according to the circumstances. It sometimes happened that a child would only open up "and reveal some pertinent information" which could "provide clues for tracing" after having become accustomed to the environment and feeling sufficiently relaxed.[221] The caregivers therefore needed some time in assisting the young residents "to trust the team, to talk to them and to believe that supreme efforts would be made to find their parents and relatives."[222]

Many of the Polish, Yugoslavian and Czechoslovakian children had spent several years in Germanization programs under the influence of pro-nationalist adults and had not used their mother tongue. And even once the war had ended, they had not been permitted to return home. Some were unsure of their nationality but believed and insisted that they were German. Only after they had spent a considerable amount of time in the Children's Center did they feel free enough to reveal their thoughts and doubts.[223] Thus, a group who arrived from St. Joseph's Children's Home in Kaufbeuren claimed at first to be German. After having spent a few days at Indersdorf, however, they approached visitors with smiles, greeted them in Polish and declared themselves unwilling to return to Kaufbeuren.[224] It was impossible for the UNRRA team to check whether such groups of youths were UN nationals. But since these "displaced children" were obviously deeply worried about the fates of their families, longing for news from them and urgently wanting to go home, they were helped to learn and speak the language that was most useful to achieve the desired reunion with their families. Lists with these children's names would then be given to the various national liaison officers in order to trace their parents.

When individual German youths pretended to be foreigners in order to receive DP status, peers would usually unmask them immediately. They would then be transferred to German institutions. Other Gentile youths who tried to claim Jewish identity in order to be classified as "stateless" and thus not repatriated to their home countries would also be quickly recognized by young survivors.[225] They had a knack for uncovering hidden identities, and the UNNRRA staff had a hard time stopping the accompanying acts of violence.

Marion E. Hutton and her colleague are writing down details about Zofia and Janusz Karpuk's background to send it to UNRRA's Central Tracing Office. But no relatives were found. In summer 1946 the children returned to Poland and grew up in an orphanage.

If it proved impossible to establish citizenship or nationality with certainty, the case was sent for further investigation to the verification commission to which the zone-accredited liaison officer was attached.[226]

The team wanted the young people to join the ethnic group in which they felt most comfortable. However, Greta Fischer's detailed description of fifteen-year old Gyula makes the difficulty clear. When he arrived at Indersdorf, he claimed to be Hungarian. But when he was placed in a camp for Hungarian citizens, he came back after three days "weeping and pleading for readmission to the center. He was so disturbed that he was permitted to remain until further investigation might reveal a more suitable placement."[227] In the meantime, he had begun insisting that he was really Czech, not Hungarian, and succeeded in producing enough proof to make this believable. His case, however, couldn't be decided in Indersdorf and was therefore sent on to the Czech Liaison Officer for approval.[228]

Liaison officers from various nations visited the Children's Center to determine which youngsters could be sent back to their home countries, but each applied a variable approach. For instance, one would accept any child who offered plausible information about his home of origin whereas another insisted on incontrovertible proof of citizenship – which in most cases was impossible to procure. A third rejected out of hand all children with German-sounding names.[229] Fights about whether a child was Polish or Russian occurred.[230] The team disagreed with the Soviet liaison officer when he wanted to repatriate to Russia a group of children who clearly belonged in Upper Silesia.[231] True, such decisions were often complicated by the lack of identification papers. Children and adolescents were asked to supply their nationality, place of birth, place of residence and native language; they were also requested to state whether relatives had served in a particular army. Given the child's age, the answers would be correspondingly interpreted. How names were spelled would be considered as well as how the children were brought to Germany. If someone described being forcibly removed from home, this child was presumably not German. The names of certain refugee centers, such as "Klosterbrück" in Upper Silesia, indicated that the adolescent girl or boy had been trafficked through a collection point for "stolen children."

Those — like fourteen-year-old Anna — who feared their parents were dead or who had already attended an Upper Silesian German school for six years preferred to remain in Germany. Greta Fischer described Anna as a "confused, disturbed child" who often complained about various pains and had fainting spells. However, "since she attached herself to the Polish group and participates in their festivities, she's calmed down a bit."[232] The team understood the "process of renationalization" as an opportunity for the child to attain emotional stability and regain a sense of his or her own identity. But no one should be repatriated against his or her will. Due to their having become "Germanized,"[233] it was only with great patience and care that some youth could be persuaded to return to their homelands. "There were some children, relatively few in number, who expressed interest in remaining in Germany. They were chiefly those who had been strongly 'Germanized' and felt very ill at ease among members of their own national group, had trouble with the native language and were unfamiliar with national customs."[234] In such cases, the UNRRA contract's mandate for "quick repatriation" could not be fulfilled, and the Children's Center had to be their more permanent refuge. Marion E. Hutton, deputy director, came to the conclusion, "The main hope of those of us in charge of the children was to give them a home. We worked not only for their physical welfare. Although we could not completely supply the greatest need of the individual child – that of home relations – we tried to approximate it. Our entire program and everything we did was for the welfare of the child rather than for the convenience of national governments, agencies or personnel of the center."[235]

Because a quota of 50 young people from Indersdorf had permission to enter England as long as they were under 16, UNRRA staff produced the occasional birth certificate with a lower birth date.[236] "We were sympathetic to helping them to make themselves younger."[237] When sometime later the Canadian government agreed to accept Jewish youths under 18, Greta Fischer was caught helping out, "I think I must have been very honest when a Canadian offer arrived and a Canadian social worker visited Kloster Indersdorf. I candidly shared my concern with her that some of them were probably older than the papers showed. She became very, very angry with me and told me that this was totally unacceptable."[238] Still, for those in daily contact with the young survivors, care for the benefit they would derive from individual attention in a foster family outweighed absolute honesty. "The UNRRA team often found itself in conflict over rules and directives that had to be observed. ... It must be admitted that the human element usually won out."[239]

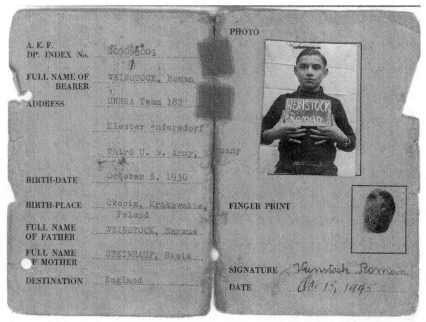

Roman Weinstock's UNRRA ID card from Kloster Indersdorf. He was born in 1927 but the ID shows a birthdate allowing his immigration to England.

Searching for relatives who might have survived

The young people conversed a lot about their experiences in the camps but among themselves, one topic was never mentioned: "Although we were discussing our past, no one was willing to talk about their nearest and dearest. Secretly we were deluding ourselves [into believing] that one day we would meet perhaps by chance and hopefully soon. This hope was held even by those who already knew the fate of their loved ones."[240]

Staff fed the young people's hopes when asking them to make their personal information as detailed as possible so that missing notices could be successful. "Maybe tomorrow we'll find your parent with the help of details in your document."[241]

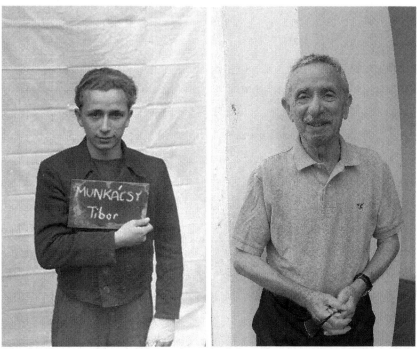

The bandage at Tibor's left hand resulted from his tangible defense against anti-Semitic insults by Gentile teenagers. Today he lives as Tibor Sands in New York City.

The initiative of the children themselves in actually locating relatives "was phenomenal," Greta Fischer wondered.[242] When on September 30, 1945 the Czech film director Hanus Burger and the Jewish-German writer and journalist Curt Riess made a film on life at Kloster Indersdorf,[243] they talked with some of the children about their experiences. Tibor Munkácsy asked them if they had ever heard about his half-brother Martin Munkácsi, who had emigrated from Hungary to the United States and become a famous fashion photographer. When Tibor mentioned the name, the film director "jumped with astonishment and delight." ... "Cables flew back and forth and arrangements were set in motion to arrange for admission to the United States and the start of a new life."[244]

A journalist queries survivors in Kloster Indersdorf (center left: Walter Hahn).

Furthermore, in mid-October 1945, to promote the search for missing family members, the professional American photographer Charles Haacker was commissioned to take snapshots of all children living in Kloster Indersdorf holding name plates.[245] Today most of the survivors remember this important event or know the precise story behind what they were wearing for the photo shoot: a bed sheet hanging on the wall provided a neutral background; Hans Neumann interrupted his football match to have his picture taken; Salek Benedikt, a talented artist, was asked to write the children's names in chalk on the boards; Kurt Klappholz assisted the photographer and made friends with him;[246] and Lazar Kleinmann had Greta Fischer to thank for organizing his stylish suit trousers. The children projected their hopes onto these photos that, if they were still alive, their relatives would be alerted to their whereabouts by the picture and would rush to Indersdorf and pick them up there. In a few cases this actually happened; but within most of the Jewish children dark suspicion grew gradually into horrible certainty, that from now on each was all alone in the world.[247]

"Once the hunger in their bellies was stilled, they became aware of another hunger, a gnawing pain for parents and for brothers and sisters."[248] The youngsters were restless and couldn't just sit around doing nothing. They wanted to take action themselves. To find their relatives and exchange news, the staff felt obliged to permit their charges to visit transit camps or DP meeting points such as the German Museum in Munich. And a number of these expeditions actually brought the desired result, a reunion with parents or distant relations. The stories in turn gave other youngsters hope, and right away, they wanted to do the same thing. [249]

Wolf Witelson was the only survivor of his family, while Josef Lichtenstein could be reunited with his brother Arthur in England.

Even the most impossible-seeming tips and hopes had to be followed-up. Caregivers were thoroughly astonished at the drive to act, their communication channels, and the wealth of ideas the teens came up with when searching for their relatives: "Just imagine, somebody would sit in a lorry and would see somebody in the street and would shout to him, 'I've seen your cousin!' And a lot of times, it was true. They would then go after the direction and would find somebody. They would call it the 'Displaced Person's Newspaper', everything by word [of] mouth."[250] Kloster Indersdorf was becoming better known all over southern Germany as the place where DPs from other camps could look for their "lost children." Almost every day a stream of displaced persons made their way to the convent doors in the hope that a lost relative would be found there. Thus "incredible reunions" actually took place, yet so many who found no one experienced great pain.[251]

Most Jewish children thought that if their parents or siblings had survived, they would have gone back home. Therefore they wanted to set out right away for Central or Eastern Europe, even if they had to make their own way and check out the situation by themselves. Even though the UNRRA team feared for their safety, they simply couldn't stop the highly motivated, if foolhardy, youngsters from setting out, as Greta Fischer admitted, "The children were very, very restless; ... and we became very anxious [about letting] them go. But there was no way of keeping them. No way!"[252] The center staff therefore sent them off with stamped papers and food. They received small backpacks with their names on them so that "people would know they'd come from Kloster Indersdorf, and off they went."[253] Sometimes, indeed, they returned with the news that they had found someone. "Not always their parents, but a brother or sister."[254] But often the search was in vain and many were bitterly disappointed. Greta Fischer was astonished: "The children, even the girls, have no concern about traveling without proper papers or crossing frontiers. Most of them have returned to the center and tell stories of walking through forests at night in order to by-pass frontier guards, of not being able to obtain food without ration cards, of traveling in cattle cars in inclement weather. However, they seem to be inured to such conditions and tell the story as one might describe any normal happening."[255] One Jewish girl, Suri Lachmanowicz, for instance, found her home destroyed and had to return to Indersdorf without having found her father.[256] Leon Kniker, back home in Poland, found nothing more than a family photo and a couple of other things.[257]

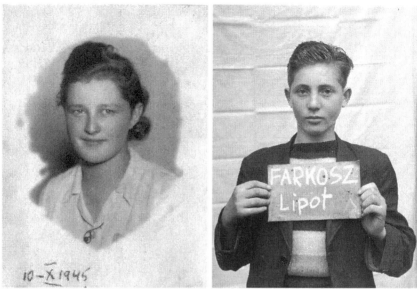

Both Suri Lachmanowicz from Czechoslovakia and Zoltán (Lipot) Farkas left Indersdorf in search for relatives who may have survived. They returned from their daring trips without any success.

Sixteen-year-old Lazar Kleinman hoped that of his ten-member family he would discover at least his sister in a clinic in Prague, but shortly before he got there she had died of an infection. As a very sad young man he returned alone to Indersdorf.[258] His childhood friend Zoltán (Lipot) Farkas made it all the way back to his Romanian hometown of Satu Mare to see if anyone else had returned and dug up buried family photos and valuables. The trip to the Carpathians was "relatively simple," he found, because he managed to cling to the outside of a cargo train. "Our house in Romania was still there. I met distant relatives and friends who had also survived – but no children or older people. Survivors were all between 16 and 30." Getting back to Indersdorf, however, was not so easy. "I had to cross seven borders. From Romania into Hungary, from Hungary to the Russian Zone and then to Austria, etc."[259] Zoltán had to bribe border guards, and with a group of Jewish refugees presumably led by the Brichah,[260] he spent a short time in jail before he could continue his journey and return to his brother Erwin and friend Lazar in Indersdorf. There he gave the two the devastating news that he had been unable to find any of their close relatives.

Sometimes it happened – for instance, to the Czech boy Pavel[261] – that a returnee would be back with no word of his loved ones but with a number of other orphaned children in tow. The team saw this as a compliment, a sign that the youngsters took it for granted that these newcomers would be "welcomed and well taken care of."[262]

Conflicts

How much educational guidance is needed?

When child survivors look back today on their condition after liberation, many of them would describe their situation in this way: "When I was maybe 13, or 15 or 18, I had nothing: no parents, no siblings, no food, no clothes, no health, only two, four or five years of schooling and no idea of how my life was going to go."[263] Many who had resided in the cloister at that time would offer a similar description. Abram Leder remembered that when he was liberated, he had nothing but his striped camp uniform from Flossenbürg and not a shimmer of certainty or even any idea of his future.[264] On the plus side of his life at that time, Maier Reinstein could recall only that he wanted to leave Germany for Eretz Israel[265] at any price.[266] Compared to adult survivors, the youngsters hadn't had a chance to develop their inner resources or moral strengths by dint of experience.[267] The Allies' team of psychologists therefore warned the staff of the D.P. camps that they would most likely have to deal with survivors' "intensified aggression, reduced sense of political responsibility and a strong propensity to steal and defy rules."[268] In fact, the Children's Center was not entirely free of this phenomenon, so that the UNRRA staff understood their work, to a certain extent, as a "re-education for life," as André Marx observed: "It's very hard but also gratifying to help these kids return to an orderly path when some of them hold the crudest ideas about life given that violence deprived them of their youth and opportunity to enjoy a well-ordered, normal development. In some, as a result of everything they witnessed in the camps, there is an attitude that requires timely, thorough, energetic and understanding intervention to prevent not only seriously disadvantaging the young people themselves but also to avoid negative consequences for society as a whole."[269]

When the *Süddeutsche Zeitung* reported on "The Children of Indersdorf" in December 1945, they featured the twelve-year old Pole "Toddy." He "was a thief when he arrived from Dachau concentration camp, where he had 'marked time' for nine months. He stole bread, hid it in his bed and slept on it. Today he no longer steals even if a certain shyness still plays around his eyes. 'Our favorite game', the little prisoner explains, was this: 'We'd crawl under a pile of corpses and move the arms to startle passers-by. It was really funny! It looked like a 'Heil Hitler' or a 'bottoms up'."[270]

How were kids with such apocalyptic backgrounds to relearn the values of normal human interaction? Their counselors had to believe that despite all odds the young people's ethical sensibilities had survived their destructive experiences. Indeed, "Although I had spent three years in German concentration camps, I hadn't lost my sense of morality," Kurt Klappholz stated forty years later.[271]

A great deal of boasting went on in these youthful communities. In the world of these children and adolescents, not success, not character, but experience of the lowest depth, survival of the most frightful ordeals, won prestige. Leadership was the prerogative of those who experienced the worst horrors or had been in captivity the longest. Those who knew only a little of what went on in the Nazi camps were written off. Indeed, these children often appeared [to believe] that people who hadn't been interned ... knew little about the realities of life.[272]

But in fact, various youngsters reacted very differently to what had been done to them. Some were passive and depressed but others wild, careless and insubordinate. Most appeared torn, restless and full of contradictions. They longed for the security they had known in their parental homes but at the same time revealed a strong sense of independence and superiority that constituted a real challenge to their counselors. On the one hand they exhibited childlike curiosity and inexperience; on the other, however, the camps had made them into "old people"[273] by what they had put them through. Many understood neither discipline nor behaviors of "normal" boys and girls, were physically and psychologically grown up and no longer children, yet curious, hopeful, emotionally torn, restless and frustrated.[274]

For instance, eighteen-year-old Moszek Sztajnkeler, a Jew from Poland, had been persecuted for nearly six years and had lost his entire family. After liberation he lived for a time with a group of young survivors in an empty house near Schwandorf. Armed with pistols, they stole watches and bicycles from German soldiers and SS men and sold these on the black market in order to buy food. Later, Moszek and a friend traveled on their own back to Poland where their black marketeering landed them in jail. Someone like Moszek would only have come to the Children's Center in the hope of finding a relative or an opportunity to emigrate to a better world. For him there was only one authority – himself. He didn't allow anyone to make the rules for him. He knew that under no circumstances would he return to a DP camp to live because it limited his movements and reminded him of the concentration camps. The Children's Center, in this sense, seemed not at all like a DP camp. Instead, he experienced Indersdorf as "a nice place" under normal conditions where his group received good medical care before traveling on to England.[275]

Moszek Sztajnkeler (Morris Stein) (2nd from right in 1st row) with his Indersdorf friends in a Jewish Children's home in Northampton, UK, in 1946. Some are still wearing the white pullover they received on entering Kloster Indersdorf.

It wasn't always easy for the staff to deal with the "superiority complex" of these teens. "The Team members would be constantly reminded that these children's experience had made them mature far earlier because they were forced to function, for survival, on an adult level,"[276] Greta Fischer wrote in her report. Later she would compare her experience as a thirty-five-year-old social worker with the lives of these youths: "Many times I think about myself, how I was then. I was young, I wanted to do good. ... I wanted to help. But in many respects their experience of life was so much more vast than mine – to go through the camps and all the horrible experiences."[277] She admired these young survivors, hungry for life, was fascinated by their unwavering belief in their own strength and saw that behind many of their behaviors lay a basic "will to survive," an "indescribable rage to live," that had been tested in the extremity of the Holocaust. "You must understand: those who survived, and especially the Jewish children, were really extraordinarily strong people. Their will to survive and their rage to live had blocked out absolutely everything else. That's the way they overcame really everything."[278]

Greta Fischer understood their rejection of authority, their tendency to emotional outbursts, their failure to observe rules and the intensive longing of these youth for personal possessions. That's why they had survived! "How can we apply our own understanding of ethics to them?" Fischer asked, and urged openness in place of moralizing.[279] If the staff wanted to help the survivors, this could be done only in cooperation with them.

At the same time, many of the youngsters displayed a "compulsive need" to "provoke anger or run foolish risks" just to convince themselves "that in spite of everything they will survive."[280] Today survivors swap a host of postwar stories of times they once again found their lives in danger. In Weiden, Miklos Roth, for instance, nearly drowned in his first attempt to swim.[281] Imre Hitter, newly released from the hospital in Neunburg vorm Wald, was taking his first steps from the building when he saw a horse. Standing too near its hindquarters, he received a massive kick that sent him straight back to the clinic. Today both Roth and Hitter feel that not only did the camps treat them in despicable ways, but they also robbed them of the normal experience of youth. "We wanted everything and more, instantaneously. We did not want to waste precious time or to be restricted by limitations. In other words, we were reckless. What could be done tomorrow, we had to do today!"[282] Whether it was bicycle stunts, riding accidents[283] or attempts to drive motorcycles or American Jeeps,[284] their behavior was not always safe. For example, when the teens returned from hiking through the woods with munitions and grenades, the staff strictly forbade it. But this degree of strictness was far from satisfactory as far as the Sisters of Mercy were concerned. As Sister Dolorosa wrote to the Motherhouse, "Our supervisors, the ladies of the UNRRA, are very good to us, but regarding the children, we have no say, and there's nothing we can do. At the slightest hint of grievances, they answer, 'Be good to the children because they've been through so much,' and they think that takes care of everything."[285] One reason for the teenagers' careless behavior, in Greta Fischer's eyes, may have been disappointed expectations of liberation: "I think this hope helped them to survive. Many had ardently hoped that the world would become their oyster but there were so many disappointments everywhere. And they were depressed, most certainly many were depressed."[286] You don't dream for years of a better world without a certain amount of idealizing. But it wasn't only hope of a better life that they had carried with them in the camps. During their convalescence immediately after the war, the Jewish youths in particular, had faced decisive psychological challenges in that a false hope had been raised of quickly finding a new and better homeland in, say, the USA. The fact that months later they were still residing in the land of the perpetrators and that they hadn't yet any idea of how their situation could change embittered some of them. Caregivers had to help them overcome their disappointment with the real situation after liberation and persuade them to utilize the delay in meaningful ways. Helpful in counteracting their depression and dissatisfaction were the staff's efforts to provide individual attention, to encourage developing their talents, to support them, talk to them and like them, even if their behavior wasn't always "good."

Yet, from time to time punishments were meted out, for instance, a day of house arrest by Greta Fischer. The resulting protest poster in artistic lettering by Roman Kniker (Kent) has been preserved.[287] Thus, Greta Fischer set limits for her charges when she deemed these appropriate, and this probably accounts for the brothers Erwin and Zoltán Farkas calling her "stricter" than other

UNRRA staffers.[288] Yet today they smile when they recall the incident and are sure it was in their best interest.

A group of Jewish boys protested against a day's house arrest. Roman Kent (Kniker), today President of the International Auschwitz Committee, created this poster against Greta Fischer's parenting style.

Suddenly discovering sexuality

Most of the young people had spent the crucial years of puberty in ghettos and camps. There they encountered not only the destruction of their families and of sex-specific gender roles, but also sexual violence and exploitation. As shaved and skeletal slave laborers they had been unable to think of themselves as woman or man, girl or boy. After liberation, many teens found recovery accompanied by an overwhelming initial discovery of their sexuality, as Kurt Klappholz confirmed. Deported at age fifteen, the permanent hunger he suffered meant "girls were no longer important."[289] In a hospital in Neunburg vorm Wald, having recovered somewhat from the strains of his death march, the eighteen-year-old found himself in a "totally sexualized atmosphere." The first sight of young nurses triggered a wholly unexpected reaction that led him – although still so weak he could hardly walk – into the first sexual adventure of his life. And what pleased him most about it was the way it radically turned the tables. Only a few days before, his relationship with this German nurse would have been punishable by death for "Rassenschande" — "defiling the race."[290] In the few weeks he spent with the American Army in Neunberg vorm Wald, he was surprised to find so many German girls and women, thoroughly demoralized, who offered themselves to their American liberators while the soldiers in large numbers ignored the rules against fraternization, especially with regard to all these available "German Fräuleins." During his delayed but therefore all the more impetuous sexual maturation, Kurt Klappholz got a German girlfriend right away at Indersdorf and even tried to have sex with her in her parents' home. The venue certainly heightened his pleasure.[291]

Five boys around a girl (to her right Bernat Zelikovits, behind her Szlama Weichselblatt).

Later, in an interview in England, as a married man and father of two sons, he remarked in detail on such extraordinary hormonal turmoil and promiscuity in those first few years after liberation and supposed that in general, many of the recently incarcerated child survivors went through the same thing – a shared phenomenon that research has neglected so far. He admits that at Kloster Indersdorf he had nothing else on his mind but chasing girls.[292]

The Sisters of Mercy were unable to comprehend this sort of behavior on the part of the teens or young adults: "Relations between boys and girls are very free if not utterly shameless."[293] As they tried to intervene, the nuns found that some individual adolescents were "pretty good but on the whole they [were] wild, crude, and above all deficient when it came to their morals."[294] They would gladly have had the group show openness to their ethical principles – but as moral guides, the children rejected them: "The kids refused everything we tried to do although for the most part they treated the Sisters with proper courtesy."[295] The nuns found themselves limited to protecting the female personnel they supervised. "It's especially difficult for the German cleaning women and other household help. They are often harassed by the bigger boys. And it has happened that a woman cleaning a bedroom was attacked by five or six boys. Complaints [to UNRRA staff] are usually brushed off with 'well, that's all these kids have ever learned or seen in Germany'. As a result, we suffer a chronic shortage of household help. No proper girl will stay." Given conditions like these, the nuns were unable to supplement the lack of custodians and cleaners. As Sister Dolorosa reported to her motherhouse, "Sometimes I get really frightened because we have a number of big girls, sixteen-year-olds, who have been ruined by life in the camps. Right away we mounted a statue of St. Joseph, to make him the patron of this house and pray to him every day, asking him to avert the evil that we are unable to prevent."[296] The Sisters implored rescue by St. Joseph, the model of chastity. They hoped that "prayer, sacrifice and repentance" would counteract unacceptable conditions in the house and saw the only real solution in giving the young people "work or repatriation."[297] In Greta Fischer's reports we find no mention of sexuality although these now grown-up boys, meeting at the annual reunions of survivors, remember with grins and good humor their discovery of the other sex. With particular enthusiasm they talk about survivor Mojze Besserman, who was remembered by his peers for a memorably pointed remark. As one UNRRA staff member challenged him for supposedly spending too much time with a Polish girl, he answered "with an unforgettable innocent face: If she loves me and I love her, what's wrong with that!?"[298] The sentence had the desired effect because the UNRRA staff member is said to have left the room, stuck for an answer.

Clashes with the German neighborhood

While suffering in the camps, most survivors had imagined that once they got out a penitent world would treat them well and punish the wrongdoers. In the first few months after the end of the war, they often lived near the US military and saw themselves in the same battle against their former tormenters. Many felt a deep hatred for the Germans. "It was extremely difficult to help the children deal with these feelings when everything in their daily lives was surrounded by the German atmosphere and when they had to continue living in Germany after the liberation. The staff of the center often wondered what damage was being caused and how the rehabilitation process was being slowed down by these factors."[299] The Children's Center sat right on the town square so that, again and again, fighting broke out between the village children and the boys and girls from the cloister who "welcomed opportunities to express retaliation and hatred,"[300] as Marion E. Hutton remarked. The caregivers – including the Sisters of Mercy – understood Jewish survivors' hatred of the Germans: "By far the largest group among the Jewish children (aged 13-20) were those who had suffered the horrors of the camps. Most of them were the sole remaining members of their families. Their mothers, their fathers, and often as many as ten to a dozen siblings, they said, had been murdered, whipped to death, incinerated etc. etc. or otherwise killed, the entire family simply exterminated. They had confronted truly frightening and horrible things and therefore they detested all Germans."[301]

This hatred expressed itself not only in plundering neighbors' gardens, but also in gratuitous vandalism: they would rip off branches and let the fallen fruit lie. The neighbors complained to the Children's Center. Greta Fischer reports how she and her colleague André Marx stood up for the children in this instance and asked the Germans to give the apples and pears to the cloister before they could be stolen or rotted. The neighbors complied and delivered the fruit to the center.[302]

This positive outcome notwithstanding, the small rural village of Indersdorf offered few opportunities to cultivate positive interaction with the local community. The attraction of the pub right opposite the convent building was the beer that was beeing served. Katalin Szász, one of the Kibbutz members, was an exception. Not only did she prefer coffee with much sugar that she brought with her from the center, she also enjoyed her contact with the locals. "Our visit there was special for me as I could be in the company of the town's people. Staying mostly among our own group, we didn't have much contact with the population. Going there by ourselves without the escort of soldiers that we were used to while in the camps, gave me the taste of freedom and a little bit the sense of liberation."[303] Most of the others would probably agree with Moshe Ganan's statement: "This Gasthaus I did also frequent. I remember very faintly the face of the bartender, but remember not having anything to do with the German population, whom, if anything, we abhorred, somewhat even feared because maybe they were after all till recently Jew-baiters."[304] The UNRRA therefore tried at least to avoid open hostilities by keeping their charges for the most part within the convent walls. As Marion E. Hutton commented, the children's living space was thus limited to inside the cloister except for occasional excursions to seek relatives and run special errands to Munich. "Prescribed life under such circumstances is difficult for adolescent boys and girls."[305]

Encounters with Germans, of course, could not be entirely avoided. "The other thing was, we had to go through Dachau when we went to Munich. Munich was the place where we processed the children later on for passports and for their papers. Whenever we went through Dachau, the boys had already their pockets full of stones and would throw the stones on the population. And although we definitely could understand them, we did not want them to spend their lives to be so hostile. So we talked to them and tried to prevent this kind of behavior."[306] The staff tried to convince the youngsters that such hatred would work to their own disadvantage and would poison their hearts. They could only help themselves by overcoming their feelings of hatred and concentrating on the positive events in their lives. But to do so, they needed time, a lot of time, as well as geographical distance. As Greta Fischer explains:

On open trucks the teenagers passed Dachau where they seized the opportunity to take "revenge."

Most of the older children reflect the fact that their present life in Germany is somewhat like living in an oasis. It is unnatural and abnormal. Their urge to grab and to dominate is a reflection not only of their experience in the past when they had so little and were so mistreated, but also a natural reaction to their present surroundings where they are forced to live in the midst of the same community that had been responsible for their suffering. Very little that is constructive can be done about this until they are removed from Germany.[307]

Should survivors help with housework?

One aim of rehabilitation was to enable the children to regain their sense of dignity and self-respect. Living in a dirty house as a welfare recipient, expected to do nothing, was not a state conducive to confidence-building. There is a social as well as a personal value of work. For that reason, the UNRRA Team 182 thought it important that the children help one another by doing household chores and taking responsibility. When tasks were assigned, a broad spectrum of reactions greeted them, but not unlike those typical of teens anywhere. It was relatively easy to find volunteers to care for the little ones or decorate the home. For instance, on Christmas 1945, the baroque dining hall and many of the dormitories had large Christmas trees. But just as in adult DP camps, Indersdorf residents debated fiercely over whether ex-camp inmates and slave laborers should be expected to work at all.[308] After considerable debate, the UNRRA team concluded that work should be considered pedagogically important. Each child and teen would be asked to "delegate one hour's work per day"; tasks conformed to the age and health of the resident.[309] Nonetheless, debate continued. "A serious shortage of cleaning personnel made it necessary to put more responsibilities on the children. We met with them to explain the situation. The results have been quite good and we have tried to stress the value of this work for their future."[310]

The UNRRA team was firmly convinced that persuasion would work better than sanctions and more or less successfully applied this philosophy, as we can gauge from a contemporary newspaper article: "Setting the table and serving are among the youngsters' chores. The head of the Children's Center, an American social worker, explained that this was not due to lack of employees but for the good of the children who needed to relearn how to care for themselves. Many had, until just recently, worked only under duress and had therefore developed a certain antipathy to work as such."[311]

DP youths assist German employees in the kitchen.

What mattered was not only self-interest, but the welfare of the whole center as one particular incident showed. One evening the young people threw a spontaneous party, but afterward nobody wanted to deal with the resulting chaos. "We're not here to clean up!" "Let the Germans do it. We were their slaves long enough!" The UNRRA team was convinced something was amiss and, as educators, intervened. Greta Fischer recalls how they gathered the kids together and let them know that the staff understood their feelings but didn't believe they should live with this hatred in their hearts. Fischer also told them that when they gave a party, they had to clean up afterward. So a "repeat performance" was planned, and the kids would clean up.[312] After all, special events could take place only if the youngsters took full responsibility. However, they were "very upset by these instructions, holding that the UNRRA team showed no understanding of the treatment they had received at the hands of the Germans and that consequently the Germans owed them a great deal of service in return. However, after such discussion and explanation that the object was not to save the labor of the Germans but rather to prepare them, the children, for life in a normal community in a free country, the children accepted the UNRRA position"[313] and planned another party that was perfectly organized. The staff didn't have to lift a finger. "So some of the things we wanted to get across to them did get across to them, that you could not live with hatred so much. But it took a long time,"[314] Fischer says. In addition, this participation in the operation of the center helped to revive the interest of the older teenagers in the life of the community and to regain initiative and responsibilty which often had been lost under Nazi subjugation.

The party at a festive table (Greta Fischer, sitting, fourth from left wearing a bowtie).

Should Jews and Gentiles be separated?

Specific challenges faced by a Children's Center housing both Jewish and Gentile youngsters became clear from the very beginning: "The Polish children, this particular group who were so indoctrinated by the Germans, the boys and girls stayed together in two big rooms. ... So one evening the conversation came, that next day a group of Jewish children was to arrive. When the Polish girls heard this, they said, they would not stay with Jewish children in one place. That all Jews were terrible people. They were Satans, they had horns, and they were afraid they would kill them all. ... It took us months, every day to go over the same story, that there were Jewish people, there were Catholic people, there were all kinds of people, and there were good and bad people. ... The re-education was a very, very difficult part."[315]

There were repeated conflicts among the many nationalities and religious groups. Language barriers as well as the fact that the kids could choose their own roommates and dining hall companions led not only to strengthening their sense of ethnic belonging, but also to exclusion of others. The greatest potential conflicts were between the Polish Catholics and Polish Jews because before the war there had already been considerable anti-Semitism in Poland. Greta Fischer repeatedly reported viewpoints expressed by Gentile children that "they found it impossible to be friendly to Jews," adding that "they were hysterical to learn that some team members were Jewish, and they repeated over and over again that it was impossible for Jewish people to treat them in a sympathetic way."[316] What better solution to this particular problem than for those who were already trusted helpers to reveal the fact that they were Jews?! Fischer felt that the "obvious identification of the youngsters with members of the multinational team" was of "inestimable value in teaching tolerance and respect for each other."[317]

Nonetheless, this lesson came only with great patience and tenacious effort to convince, as in the case of nine-year-old Alexander Pecha: "He had been the mascot of a German officer and every time he went through the corridors ... he would call 'Heil Hitler!' And the Jewish children were terribly sensitive to that. They would nearly kill the child. I wanted to enter the fight. I don't know how I got out of the fight to separate the two groups, the Jewish children and this little boy. It took a long time until we explained to this child that he could not do that."[318]

Most of the boys liked playing football. But an effort to use the sport to enhance understanding between Jews and Gentiles in a natural way failed dismally. Anti-Semitic slurs shouted out by a few Polish boys provoked such a brawl that referee André Marx was obliged to stop the game. In terms of education, the UNRRA Team 182's mandate in a center housing both Jewish and Gentile children was not only to promote the return to national and religious identity, but also to teach harmonious co-existence. This was quite a juggling act. Instruction was intended not only to restore parental values, language, tradition and customs, but also to ensure that everyday life be lead peacefully in spite of differences.

Director Lillian D. Robbins in discussion with children before they leave for convalescence in Switzerland.

From the start the team gave all religious beliefs room to develop. Already in September 1945, director Lillian D. Robbins reported that UNRRA members ran Jewish services, and Roman Catholic children attended the nearby convent church. She also wanted special services for minorities such as the Protestants and eastern Orthodox churches,[319] and in the spring of 1946, these were in fact offered at the Children's Center itself or the opportunity given to attend such services elsewhere.[320] From the beginning of 1946, Shabbat was celebrated on Friday night and Saturday in a special room in the cloister. Religious Jews, however, in Indersdorf as in the other DP camps, were a minority.[321] If religious conviction stemming from parental influence remained, events of the Shoah often acted to slacken it. Jewish survivors who revisit Indersdorf today recall heated debate about "where God was in Auschwitz." Although during schooldays in the Carpathian Mountains, Lazar Kleinmann was teased because of his side locks and to him many Orthodox Jewish rules seemed bothersome, at a moment of existential despair in Auschwitz, he talked to God and swore that if he were saved, he would attend Yeshiva for one year. In Indersdorf he had not forgotten that vow and interpreted his having been saved to God's holding up his part of the bargain. Kleinmann in turn kept his promise by attending Yeshiva in England. Many of the older kids, however, questioned the very existence of God and asked themselves which Jewish traditions to keep.

Jewish and Gentile children celebrating Purim in March 1946. (Front row with guitar: Alexander Pecha)

Because the Children's Center had been set up to accommodate various faiths, not much attention was paid either to kosher food or to other rules governing Jewish daily life. In only the rarest cases did the boys wear a yarmulke or take advantage of the option to regularly observe the Sabbath. In contrast, Jewish holidays were celebrated. It was then that Jewish youth reclaimed Jewish identity; some fasted or enjoyed Sukkoth or Purim. Manfred Heyman (Haymann)[322] remembers how on Rosh Hashanah the Sisters showed sensitivity to their Jewish charges by laying out bed sheets with which the Christian symbols in the convent's church could be covered up. Enthusiastically, he tells how he and other youths celebrated Sukkoth by removing the roof from a small building in the cloister's garden and then reconstructing it with fresh twigs.[323] Arrangements for Passover 1946 were made by the Jewish Committee in Munich for 52 Indersdorf residents and included the necessary kosher food.[324] However, unlike purely Jewish children's homes such as Strüth,[325] not all cultural and leisure activities could be arranged to remind the Jewish children of their heritage and help them to maintain or return to it.[326]

In addition to religious instruction, another aim at the cloister was to help "the children who had been forced to forget their own background" to find it again. Therefore "as many activities as possible were conducted in their native tongue."[327] If enough adult DPs could be found to teach, classes were held in the children's native languages. Songs, dances and folklore were taught so that those originally from Yugoslavia, Poland or Czechoslovakia would feel more at home once they were returned to their native lands.[328]

The girls who had been "kidnapped" from Upper Silesia were permitted, at first, to choose which language they preferred to speak, German or Polish. "But they wanted desperately to regain their Polish identities," Lillian D. Robbins wrote in a letter that ten of the girls carried with them en route to a long convalescence in Switzerland. To avoid confusion, the Swiss institution was asked not to use another language but to allow the young patients to continue their education in Polish.[329]

At Kloster Indersdorf a babel of tongues was spoken, with German as the lingua franca. Jewish survivors could speak their mother tongues quite well. "Even though they hated everything German, they found the German language their easiest medium of expression."[330] Because Yiddish was so much like German and due to their experience in German camps, they could understand and speak at least some German. The caregivers, therefore, tried, whenever possible, to use German as a bridge among the various linguistic groups including more than 20 nationalities. Thus Jewish and Gentile youth were instructed in German, and this often worked quite well.

Although adult DP teachers and instructors did not always give their full support to the centrally mandated balancing act between encouragement of cultural identity and mutual respect, they had an enormous influence in these matters on their charges. Thus, UNRRA staff would notice how good relations seemed to be among various groups only to realize, time and again, that this was superficial; seemingly out of nowhere hidden and therefore all the more violent disputes erupted. In December 1945, for instance, a Polish priest insisted that Jewish children should not be admitted to Christmas dinner because this meal was part of the religious ceremony.[331] The Jewish children felt discriminated against and protested vehemently. A decision was reached after "innumerable meetings of the entire staff, UNRRA, the DPs and the Children's Council that the Polish Catholic children have their dinner ceremony separate from all the other children, the non-Polish Catholics, the Protestants, and the Jews, and that the entire center would assemble together after the dinner for the giving of gifts, singing of carols, etc."[332] Only after extensive discussion among everyone involved and a democratic decision-making process could agreement be reached, a consensus favoring equal treatment for all. The idea that holidays should be celebrated together promoted tolerance more than national identity and difference. For that reason we can assume that Purim festivities in March 1946 also included Gentile children who dressed up and shared in the fun. To ensure peaceful coexistence, it was important that no one felt discriminated against but rather learned about the holidays and customs of the others by celebrating with them.

An UNRRA inspection committee that had visited Kloster Indersdorf repeatedly found that in November 1945, staff paid significant attention to "problems among groups and conflicts of loyalty." The result was that "an atmosphere of freedom and happiness" could be discerned.[333]

Despite existing prejudice and "conflicts that have been evident in the center," the UNRRA team continued to feel it was "very worthwhile that the children have had the experience of living together."[334] Jews and Gentiles used the same dining hall and went to the same school. Some even made friends, and the Polish girls learned to mix freely with the Jewish boys. There even blossomed a couple of romances.[335] One of the girls from Upper Silesia, Stefanie Watolla, confesses today that she would eagerly have married a Jew.[336] UNRRA staff thought that ethnic proximity was exceptionally valuable for teaching tolerance and respect. When the Harrison Report[337] appeared and urged that in the US Zone separate facilities for Jewish DPs be set up,[338] Greta Fischer was not yet ready to give up the opportunities she saw in having Jewish and Gentile children sharing the same living space: "The team did its utmost – had there been more time to do more intensive direct work with the children, probably a larger contribution to the building of a positive attitude of international understanding could have been made."[339] Marion E. Hutton, the temporary director of the Children's Center in early 1946, also saw clear signs of the good derived from youths rooming in quarters with various religious beliefs and nationalities. But given limited personnel and space, larger groups were necessarily advantaged while minorities had to do without special teachers, caregivers and classrooms. Therefore she urged giving up the "idealistic thinking" and she prefered housing homogeneous groups in locations designed to meet their particular needs.

Education and Leisure

General education

Teachers and staff in the cloister tried hard to organize time as meaningfully as possible for the residents. All girls and boys were given the opportunity to go to school, to learn trade skills and participate in organized leisure activities. The aim was to "normalize our lives,"[340] as Erwin Farkas remarked concerning the intentions of teachers and staff in Indersdorf.

Jakob Bulwa reading aloud in class. On his left arm you can see his tattooed Auschwitz number.

The UNRRA Team 182 gradually instituted compulsory schooling for five- to sixteen-year-olds of five hours a day, above all so that those who had spent years in camps with no schooling at all could catch up on the basics in reading, writing and arithmetic. At first a lot had to be improvised. Only eight rooms and a couple of common rooms could serve as classrooms. In August 1945 a social worker assigned children to various classes not according to age but according to their particular needs, previous education and mastery of language. Each class therefore had students in a broad range of ages. The pupils' social backgrounds were equally distinct. Many came from farming families; while others had parents who were skilled workers or in sales before the persecution. Very few of the pupils were illiterate, even those who hadn't held a pencil or read a book in many years and were totally unaccustomed to being in a classroom. The Gentile children and young people were supposed to return to their homelands whereas the Jewish youths looked forward to emigrating to the West or to Eretz Israel. Neither group had any idea of its future. But they had one other thing in common: "Most children were avid in their desire to learn; they were like sponges, absorbing everything."[341]

Janusz Karpuk (center, next to his sister Zofia) has already secured a fountain pen.

Given the lack of teachers and staff, it was lucky if professionals from the international aid organizations like the JOINT and ORT[342] could be engaged or if good DP lay teachers could offer instruction in general education, art, or profession-related subjects. Right from the beginning, an excellent DP gym teacher was hired. At first four Polish, one Yugoslav and one Lithuanian assistant teacher taught reading, writing, arithmetic, history, geography, music, English and Polish. They did arts and crafts, sang and played with the pupils – no matter that there was hardly any equipment. Textbooks were lacking, as were composition tablets and pencils; how could anyone know what content a lesson should have and how precisely to teach it? Everyone agreed that in case they hadn't yet been learned, reading and writing should be taught first. Otherwise, each of the lay teachers taught the students what he or she had learned in school.

Lillian D. Robbins immediately requisitioned textbooks, notebooks, blackboards, pencils, radios and above all, good teachers for Hungarian, Hebrew, English and the trades.[343]

Science class on September 29, 1945

The daily schedule in Indersdorf consisted of the following: "From 9 to 11 and from 4:15 to 6 o'clock, lessons were in progress. Polish and Hungarian children received their own instruction. Because it wasn't possible for children of all nationalities to be taught in their own languages, the rest were instructed in German. The Catholic Church taught religious education three times a week. Hebrew was planned for the Jewish kids but there were too few teachers."[344] In March 1946, when enough teachers had been found, the morning schedule was extended to 1 o'clock and now featured the Polish, German, Hebrew, Ukrainian and Yiddish languages, and for a time also Russian and Hungarian.

Alexander Pecha with modeling clay. Arts and crafts were seen as important for the development of creativity. The DP teacher Belenkyi Parnans had been an artist and theater set designer in the Ukraine.

After lunch and afternoon free time, art, carpentry, typewriting, sewing, gardening, music and piano were offered at 4 o'clock. Whoever was physically fit was required to take gym.[345] In addition, all pupils attended English classes.[346] Especially quick at learning were those who intended to emigrate to an English-speaking country, using the language to interact with both UNRRA staff and American soldiers.

An inspection of the Indersdorf Children's Center by the US Army in February 1946 praised the personnel for their "efficiency" and above all, for theater performances and excellent gymnastics instruction.[347]

Greta Fischer was equally impressed by the gym teacher's accomplishments and expressed astonishment at the level attained in singing, dancing, arts and crafts and acrobatics: "The children are amazingly talented and it seems quite remarkable that after years of hardship and repression they can express themselves creatively."[348]

Gymnastics in the garden at Kloster Indersdorf.

The relationship between pupils and teachers was not always easy, however. Kurt Klappholz, for instance, boycotted classes taught by two Poles. For one thing, the level bored him, but more significant was their anti-Semitism, to which he was unwilling to subject himself. Instead, he worked in the UNRRA office, leveraged his "few chunks of English" acquired since liberation, was glad to be in demand as a popular interpreter for the Children's Center and most of all, enjoyed being able to follow his favorite pursuit – courting the girls.[349]

It was also a challenge to deal adequately with traumatized pupils whose experiences made it difficult for them to concentrate or behave in class, not to mention the disturbed state of mind in which the teachers, also camp veterans, found themselves. Above all, care was needed in choosing teaching methods because "any minute, the soul's immense anguish could break loose."[350] As a young teacher in another DP camp warned, "We had to be very careful." Once she was about to write a Commandment on the board – to honor thy father and thy mother – when she stopped herself, realizing that the parents of nearly everyone in the class had been murdered by the Nazis. Or when at holiday time, she planned to teach the students how to write greeting cards to their families, she again caught herself about to write "Dear Mama" and instead began the letter with "Dear Friend."[351]

In July 1946 the school year ended with tests in all subjects taught. Polish children received certificates in Polish so that the year might be recognized once they returned to Poland. The other children received certificates in English that included a "general description" of the child. The high point of the first school year was the award ceremony held in the garden during a concert. Music students demonstrated their progress, the girls showed their skill in gymnastics and folk dancing, and the boys proved to be accomplished acrobats. This was followed by a three-day sports event in which girls and boys were encouraged to compete in racing, high jumping, swimming, soccer and netball, with very good results. The best teams received prizes, and the festivities ended with a dance party.[352]

Vocational training

Because no one really knew how the future was going to work out, it was hard to design an appropriate educational program. "This was kind of the situation most difficult to deal with. ... The security of the Children's Center was not enough. – what was needed was some real planning for the future."[353] During the years of suffering the young people had faith that afterward "all their dreams and hopes would come true."[354] Now the UNRRA staff had to "bring them gently back to reality." Because it was clear that they would have to stay for a while longer in Germany, the time could be optimized by offering the girls and boys the opportunity to develop their skills, uncover their talents and gauge their preferences for work. Whoever thought he or she might want to live on a kibbutz[355] in Eretz Israel could begin to acquire basic knowledge of agriculture. The home already had services for tailoring and shoe-making, skills that would serve the children well in later life; the girls and boys could learn these trades. The UNRRA team searched for artisans in various fields and found any number of adult DPs with the desired qualifications and willingness to teach. André Marx's report takes a realistic view of the problems they had to fight: "The art course has been temporarily discontinued because the teacher left the center ... We have organized a first-aid course for the older girls and rhythmic dancing for all girls. ... We were finally able to find a really competent auto mechanics teacher, who takes three groups of children each day as follows: 9:15 to 12:00 a.m., 1:15 to 3:45 p.m., and 4:30 to 6:00 p.m. ... The shoemaker was recently dismissed owing to shortage of leather and tools."[356]

Tailoring workshop. The Yiddish inscription on the wall says: Learn a trade to secure your future.

Despite scarcity, the young people in the Indersdorf Children's Center learned to "invest their energy in practical and creative work,"[357] and for months, carpentry, art, house painting, auto mechanics, typewriting and nursing care were taught. ORT ran a tailoring course. André Marx even managed to find temporary apprenticeships for individual Jewish and Polish youths for half days in Indersdorf enterprises, especially in carpenters' shops and agricultural machinery maintenance.[358] The teenagers could help to make toys for the younger children and equipment for the nurseries. The success of such practical training became evident in April 1946 at an exhibition of leather goods and metal toys the students had made. As inadequate and temporary as these courses were, they at least allowed a glimpse of what the real world of work was like, a practical link between the present and the future. The young people were motivated and had opportunities to test themselves and try harder: "These satisfactions arise from the redevelopment of initiative and the realization that satisfaction, contentment or even happiness are in fact inevitabl[y] bound up with use of initiative and with the acceptance of responsibility,"[359] as the Allies' Expert Psychologists' Group explained.

Leisure activities

The teenagers enjoy some excellent concerts.

Children too young for school played in the house or outside in the convent's garden, ran around, sang, did arts and crafts and painted.[360] But the older ones, too, were supposed to have enough time outside the classroom for games, sports, and leisure activities. First, however, the displaced children needed time to become themselves again and find a desire to play. Josef Lichtenstajn remembers that he and some other children found it difficult to sit patiently in classrooms. "They had missed out on a lot in their lives and were living free and wild in order to make up for what they had lost."[361] At first they spent most of their free time in the house, hanging out at the Indersdorf water tower (still today a popular young people's meeting point), or hiking through the woods and village. The team wanted to have another volunteer to take charge of planning activities. "Miss Fischer has this ability, but is too pressed with other responsibilities."[362] The adult DPs concerned with the after school program often thought that "there are more important things than recreation."[363] Nonetheless, board games and scouting were offered as well as dances, choir and orchestra, reading and sports teams.[364]

Jewish and Gentile children singing together (Bronislaw Wardzala, Berek Feldbaum, Czeslaw Olejniczak, Aron Swinik, Elfriede Libor, Theresa Kossok, Eli Rotenberg, Elisabeth Nieslony, Johanna Gmerek and others).

Special events also took place, such as classical concerts with works by Beethoven, Paderewski, Chopin, Rossini and Haydn, with piano, violin and cello, and on April 27 the then well-known violinist Aumeri even performed twice on his Stradivari.[365] The present-day chapel served as the theater and music hall.

Jakob Bulwa (front) and Walter Hahn playing ping pong. Among the on-lookers are Halina Bryks (right on a chair), Erwin Farkas, Miklos Roth and Herbert Hahn (behind the table).

The cloister offered a full program of enjoyable leisure activities: "The Children's Center also has a library with books in seven languages. It is managed by a boy who says the demand for books and newspapers is great but due to lack of material can be satisfied only to a point. ... Some American soldiers in the neighborhood have offered boxing lessons for the boys while the girls spend their free time with sewing and knitting."[366] The youngsters loved the presentations by mobile movie teams in the Children's Center or in Dachau; they enjoyed the theater in Munich or outings in the Alps. They came in droves to surround the only radio to hear news of the world and afterward to hold lively discussions about it.

Because Indersdorf artisans made toys and furniture for children, starting in December 1945 there was no longer any lack of toys to "throw, push or pull." The bigger children received sports equipment such as football goal posts and ping pong paddles and nets, as well as stage sets for their plays.[367] Boys in particular enjoyed competitive sports. In April 1946 a playing field outside the convent walls for American football and European football (soccer) was ready so that the DP youngsters in real football shoes kicking real balls became the envy of the village youths who managed to abscond with a football or two for their own use. In winter skiing and sledding were enjoyed on the small hill behind the convent's wall,[368] and in the warmer season children swam in Glonn creek.

Greta Fischer helps the Karpuks to pack their belongings for their trip to Switzerland.

The Children's Center Changes

The house needed constant repair: walls required paint, floors had to be laid and additional sanitary facilities acquired and installed. For the little ones a small kitchen was needed because, for months, meals had had to be carried on trays from the ground floor to the third. As the extremely cold winter of 1945/46 approached, thirty new heating units were indispensable if rooms were to be close to adequately warmed.[369] In this cold season when activities were mainly carried out indoors, even that big building proved much too small. Located on the village square, the venue was also "not set up to promote the development of friendly community relations."[370] Despite extreme scarcity immediately following the war, the UNRRA team was compelled to provide in the best possible way for the children's care. "In establishing the center we were obliged to meet a unique need under unique circumstances."[371] Thus the UNRRA team looked for light bulbs in the ruins of empty houses so that the cloister would not be pitch black at night[372] and struggled with catastrophic transportation and communication: "The problem of transportation has been difficult, even dangerous for a children's center. It has been almost impossible to secure proper vehicles or to maintain them in good repair through regular channels. Time and again one has had to ask some unrelated tactical unit for a needed part or some repair service as a favor because regular services that should have been available to the team were inadequate or lacking. Practically all of the work has been done through the initiative of individual team members and not as a planned service. Shopping around for automobile equipment is a time and gas consuming activity and one that should not be added to the responsibilities of an already overburdened team."[373] It was a similar nuisance to acquire potties for toilet training: "I got the first from an American major who had acquisitioned for me glass potties from a German institution. I was happiest for this gift. But the glass potties broke in due time. ... So what do you do next?"[374]

The Indersdorf Children's Center was certainly better provisioned than camps mainly for adults. Nonetheless, what was sent from overseas – powdered milk and canned goods – had to be supplemented by locally grown products like milk, eggs, fruit, vegetables, bread and meat either from the cloister's own farm or the immediate neighborhood. But this was not so easy: "The messing program has been superior to that of most D.P. centers in Germany but it is not yet entirely suitable for children. Quantitatively it is good. Although vitamins are being administered, more fresh fruits and vegetables should be served. More sugar and fats are needed. Fresh milk and meat should be provided. Children's centers should be authorized to secure these foods that are suitable for the diets of children."[375] The American directives strictly forbade local buying, but in order to enhance the stock, the UNRRA team members ignored these directives against doing business with Germans and therefore were able to acquire what was needed without bureaucratic delay and thereby saved money, time and effort.[376] In their uniforms, Greta Fischer and André Marx knocked on neighborhood doors and succeeded in convincing village people to sell them fresh food and artisans to use their skills to make up the shortfall.[377]

Need can't wait. If you need baby bottles or potties, you need them at once.

Furthermore, the Children's Center profited at first from the many American soldiers who had a heart for children. "In the early days of the project, when UNRRA Food Headquarters were scarcely felt at the field level, dealing with the military was most effective."[378] When in spring 1946, however, the UNRRA increased its involvement, procurement in the children's interests became more difficult. "Because transfer of responsibility affected all American occupied zones, the UNRRA managed provisions and care for DPs with an eye less focused on local and more on global needs."[379] Applications were now being regularly returned with the comment that the desired material could not be delivered and that there would be no point in renewing the request. But want could not wait. "When one needs baby bottles or potties one needs them immediately; when there is a need for personnel, life does not go on blissfully along without. ..."[380]

The UNRRA Team 182 found that the Children's Center could best be run if management had direct access to the decision-makers immediately responsible for them. When finally an UNRRA Supply Officer in charge of all children's camps was assigned an office in the cloister, delivery gaps could be nearly closed,[381] to everyone's great satisfaction. "We did however succeed in establishing access to higher Headquarters and later on, we were being involved in decision-making and in the formulation of policy for the benefit of other centers."[382]

Significant fluctuations

In the beginning, the members of UNRRA Team 182 threw themselves into the work at hand, adapting to "the needs of the moment without relation to the overall needs beyond their control."[383]

Indeed, many outside factors influenced management of the Children's Center. When the unusually long winter of 1945/46 appeared, the representatives of Czechoslovakia, France, Poland and the Soviet Union told the team that due to lack of heated transportation, repatriation would have to be postponed to the spring.[384] An inter-Allied agreement required for repatriation that heated transport be available.[385] The UNRRA had expected to solve the repatriation problem quickly, but now for most of the residents there was no immediate solution in sight. In January 1946, Greta Fischer wrote an update on the center's achievements to that time:

"361 children have been admitted to the D.P. Children's Center since its inception in July. Of these 50 have been sent to England, 30 to Switzerland,[386] and 18 repatriated to Yugoslavia. The average attendance is 200, there being some turnover on an individual basis. Fifty children are under three years of age, about eight between four and twelve years. The vast majority are between 14 and 16 years old."[387] At the same time, an unexpected stream of displaced children and youth kept on showing up. When the new director Jean Margaret Henshaw noticed that German institutions and other DP camps were trying to send their criminal or mentally ill cases to Indersdorf, she had the Child Welfare Supervisor in the US Zone certify that the Children's Center was an "Assembly Center" exclusively responsible for "care until repatriation or emigration of unaccompanied foreign children" and not for "child protection cases," "children of unmarried mothers" who wished "to retain custody of the child for the time being," psychotic cases or delinquent children.[388]

Children being fetched to spend some time of recovery in Switzerland.

On the one hand, Indersdorf housed a large contingent of long-term residents, but on the other hand, many stayed for only a couple of days or weeks.[389] The team was happy, for example, that a group of thirty Slovak girls and boys between eight and seventeen were able to gather for a couple of weeks in Indersdorf before they were repatriated to Slovakia on March 11, 1946.[390] But the quality reputation of the Children's Center had spread, and as a result, in early 1946 a part of it had become, practically speaking, a transit camp. Many children and teens were sent for only a few days to Indersdorf, receiving their travel documents and clothing for repatriation or emigration. But soon the clothing warehouse emptied and couldn't be replenished so quickly. The team felt overwhelmed and didn't see why preparation for further travel couldn't be undertaken where the children had previously been housed or why both caregivers and youngsters should be subjected to this additional nuisance.[391] For a short time, the fluctuation was so great that the social work unit in Indersdorf had to ask their UNRRA superiors either to provide the transients with papers before sending them over or permit them to stay for at least a week to take care of all the formalities; otherwise neither medical exams could be completed nor I.D.s for further travel produced.[392]

Screening teams[393] apparently preferred to continue sending older Polish, Yugoslav and Belgian youth to Indersdorf, whose degree of "Germanization gave cause for alarm." Here the team depended on the cooperation of national liaison officers to avoid repatriating anyone against his or her will and to ensure that proper personnel was sent to help with a sensitive renewal of the corresponding language and culture.[394]

On a typical day in 1946, you could count 312 children in care; the largest groups consisted of 113 Poles and 43 Hungarian Jews. To the surprise of the staff, throughout 1946 foreign babies and toddlers kept arriving at the convent. They came from all directions: from other institutions and from private households, so-called "foster parents." In July 1946, for instance, several severely neglected half-starved two- and three-year-olds showed up; they could not yet stand up or speak a word. But infants, too, were being brought, who had been born after the end of the war. Sometimes babies born to foreign mothers and American soldiers stationed in Germany were given up.[395]

Zofia Karpuk (with bag in her hand) and other children board a Red Cross car for their leisure stay in Switzerland.

For the smallest children, care in the cloister was only the second-best solution. Because a real family would offer better individual care to compensate for the damage caused by "physical and emotional starvation,"[396] the staff tried to place the youngest as quickly as possible, for example, in French foster families. The UNRRA felt it important that this care be long term and under sufficient supervision and control. Greta Fischer insisted, "Every caution should be taken to guard these children against any relaxation of child care standards and especially possible exploitation."[397] The youngest were wanted all over the world. Press reports had even reached America resulting in US citizens' applying to adopt Indersdorf's babies.[398] "Some German families wanted to adopt little children, which was possible, made possible. But all the countries wanted their children, Czechoslovakia, Poland, Norway, Estonia – all those countries wanted their children."[399] Where choices were to be made, however, regarding care, Greta Fischer placed the welfare of the individual child above any ideological considerations. When German foster parents applied to adopt a baby, it could be quite difficult to determine the best interests of the child. Whenever nationality and identity remained unclear, she thought it better to prefer adoption into a normal family, even if German, rather than to place the infant in a state-run institution. Yet, because at war's end the German future did not look bright, she wondered whether becoming a German wouldn't constitute a true handicap with which the little one should not be burdened.[400]

Marion E. Hutton with Jewish survivors in the inner courtyard of Kloster Indersdorf. From the left Wladislaus Fischer, Nina Krieger, Roman (Abraham) and Hermann (Zwi) Weinstock, Marion E. Hutton, Sacher (Steve) Israeler, Moszek Sztajnkeler (now Morris Stein), Dezider Kahan, Henryk Weinberg.

In January 1946 Greta Fischer expressed the opinion that "these children require another year of special care in order to be fully rehabilitated. Such care could be continued in Germany under the auspices of UNRRA or some other international service agency. The important factor is not the location but the quality of personnel and the adequacy of supplies."[401] The children also needed reliable care: "Changes of venue should, however, be kept to a minimum and occur only when we can be sure that the new environment is an improvement over the old."[402]

For fifty Jewish youths in Indersdorf, the big change took place at the end of October 1945. They were accepted by Great Britain. "Our wish has been granted, we'll be off to England soon/we heartily thank the UNRRA/for our good fortune,"[403] as Kurt Klappholz rhymed in his song of thanks to the team. Shortly before departure, to which everyone avidly looked forward, the mood was emotional and contradictory, anticipation mixed with pain of good-byes, nostalgia and envy. It was therefore an especially happy but also sad day when, on October 15, fifty Jewish survivors received their UNRRA identity cards permitting them to leave for England. The event gave all Jewish DPs hope that soon other opportunities to emigrate would open up. But when their paths parted, friends found the separation especially painful and enacted dramatic scenes. Many had the feeling that the rest of their lives were now being determined by smaller or greater coincidences or stumbling blocks, the fact that some were bound for England, others for Israel or the USA. Salek Benedikt lamented, "Sadly, two from our group had to stay behind because they were diagnosed with tuberculosis. Both had been good friends of mine, Berek Feldbaum and Naftali Steinberg,[404] the gentlest people I had ever known."[405] To the staff's great regret, not only illness but also age barriers could separate friends: "One of the saddest situations the UNRRA team was confronted with was when two brothers – one of them over 16 – and their best friend, 15, were separated because the friend could take advantage of the invitation to go to England and the brothers could not because one of them was over age."[406]

The Reinstein brothers were also prevented from going to England when two of their older sisters were found alive; the four eventually emigrated together to Israel. But in contrast, Moszek Sztajnkeler and Abram Warszaw were overjoyed by the surprising news that they would be pushed up from the waiting list and thereby became, years later in English speaking countries, Morris Stein and Alec Ward.[407]

Siblings should stay together, if possible.

When the group of fifty Jewish youths was finally ready to embark in October 1945, hurdles remained. They were driven a number of times, in vain, to Munich Airport. One time the plane wasn't ready; then it was fog that prevented lift-off; a third time, the truck that was to transport the children accidentally went over an embankment. After four postponements, the group finally took off on October 31, 1945. Kurt Klappholz, Salek Benedikt, Sinaida Grussmann, Bernat Nasch, and Alfred Buchführer were among the lucky ones flying from Munich to Southampton. Josef Lichtenstajn remembers that many had bread in their pockets because they did not know if they had anything to eat the next day.[408] Martin Hecht had stones in his pockets because he imagined that he could drop them off the plane onto Germany.[409] For all of them it was the first time traveling by plane. For their entire lives, the Hecht brothers, Imre Hitter and most of the others saved the farewell letter from the cloister's director: "On the day we left, the director, Lillian Robbins, handed each of us a personal letter. And so we said good-bye to all those lovely people who really did care. I am still thankful for the good fortune to have met them,"[410] Salek Benedikt would note 55 years later.

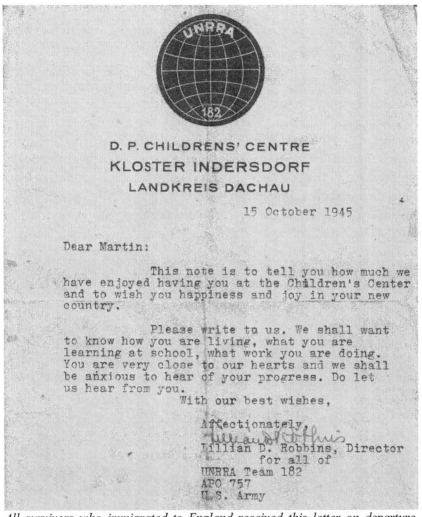

All survivors who immigrated to England received this letter on departure. Many of them stayed in touch with members of UNRRA Team 182.

A good number of the travelers responded to Lillian D. Robbins' request for news and reported on the exciting events: "We flew off, landed at Southampton and were greeted by the people who were subsequently to look after us. Shouts of Shalom and we got a certain sense of relief at having arrived. I don't know why we were given dolls and toys on arrival. I was by then eighteen and a half and I was by no means the oldest in the group; there were chaps of 22 or 20 and 24."[411] Obviously little was known about the group, as the "diapers, towels and small children's toothbrushes" revealed.[412] Nonetheless, enthusiasm was hardly lessened. "We were brought to a grand mansion called Wintershill Hall and I fell in love with England, ... the countryside, the beautifully tended hedges, lawns, the immaculate roads, the English cobblestone."[413] Among the fifty survivors who had gone to England were two Polish-Jewish refugees with a different history of persecution that had led them there via Indersdorf. Already in September 1945, nine-year-old Chaim and his eleven-year-old brother Aron Swinik had been brought by their stepmother to Kloster Indersdorf after they had survived the Holocaust together in the Soviet Union but were forced to flee from anti-Semitism once again on returning to their Polish home.[414]

Nine-year-old Chaim Swinik and his eleven-year-old brother Aron survived the Shoa in the Soviet Union.

In the first half of 1946, among those who continued to stream into Indersdorf were not only small children and "strongly Germanized" youths, but also Jewish survivors who had been hidden or had passed with "Aryan identities." They were accustomed to living precarious existences in which the slightest mistake could have life or death consequences. And even if to a certain extent they had continued to enjoy more or less normal social interaction, they were physically and spiritually scarred. After years living double lives, it was a challenge for them to find a place in any group. For instance, there were the seven siblings who arrived in April 1946 in Indersdorf. The nuns reported that the youngest, Renée, had turned six but was no taller than a three-year-old. The others, at seven, nine, twelve, fourteen, seventeen and nineteen were also very undernourished. During the war a family in East Prussia had pretended that all seven were their own relatives. "Certainly a daring gesture, fourteen-year-old Ruth said, as their tiny farm was on a lively road and could be seen by any number of SS and party members. Naturally the poor farmer had nothing to offer the children, having so little himself, so the children had to work. The fourteen-year-old mainly tended the younger ones while the oldest, a melancholy soul, was continually preoccupied with thoughts of suicide."[415] Their mother had died in a concentration camp while their father survived only to be killed early in 1946 in a car accident. These were the first children to receive visas for the USA.[416]

Sixteen-year-old Szlama Weichselblatt also looked back on a wholly different history of persecution than the camp survivors. Like the Swinik brothers he can be seen as a forerunner of the major Jewish flight from pogroms in Poland and other Eastern European countries that began at the end of 1945 and reached their high point in 1946.[417] Szlama had survived the Holocaust living in caves in the Ukraine; his mother, brother and most of his relatives had been murdered. When in April 1944 his small group of "living skeletons" emerged into the daylight for the first time in nearly two years — the longest recorded instance of uninterrupted cave habitation known[418] — they were unable to keep their eyes open, and their Russian liberators commented that it would be kinder to shoot them. Szlama, however, returned to his village to find not a single Jewish member of his community alive as well as his house empty and half destroyed, but he managed to take away a few hidden family photos. After spending some time working on farms, he heard that the UNRRA in Germany helped the persecuted to leave Europe. So he set out for Munich. It was bitter cold, he was in rags and hadn't been able to clean himself for months when he arrived at the *Deutsches Museum*, a popular DP meeting point. There he met a couple of boys who looked quite well-dressed and he asked them where they came from. They told him about the D.P. Children's Center in Indersdorf, but refused to take him there because "it was filled." They were going to the movies, but to Szlama this sounded like they were "going to the moon." When the boys were picked up by a truck, he also climbed up, but was forced to go down again. Fortunately, his desperate situation ended: "Suddenly a guy grabbed my shoulder and said, "Don't worry, you go"," Szlama recollects this turning-point of his life. On their way to Indersdorf, he couldn't believe his eyes, when the other survivors were throwing stones and smashing windows while passing Dachau. When he arrived at the convent's office, he burst out, "You can't throw me out, my father is an American citizen!" The UNRRA welfare officer Helen Steiger answered, "Who told you that stupid story; we are here to help you!" Szlama was sure that the bath he received then was the first within a year.[419] For Greta Fischer, it was evident that not only good luck but more important, Szlama's "will to survive" and "rage to live" had allowed him to come through unimaginable cruelties.[420] Even though his fate had been quite different from most of the children, he integrated very well and was quickly one of the best-liked members of the Jewish group whom others admired as an especially "strong fellow."[421] Szlama actually located his father in the USA, but due to strict American immigration quotas, he had to wait till July 1946 for permission to join him.[422]

The young Jewish refugees from Central and Eastern Europe who came to Indersdorf in 1946 were mainly not concentration camp survivors like those who had arrived first. Some of the older ones had fought as partisans against Nazi troops while younger ones had – thanks to a considerable amount of luck – survived under pitiful conditions in parts of the Soviet Union not occupied by German troops. After they had returned to their homelands where they faced new outbreaks of anti-Semitism and had no means of support, they joined Zionist organizations and together with their Madrichim[423] made their way through Czechoslovakia and Austria to the American Zone. They hoped they could more easily emigrate from there to Israel. Most were orphans; in cases where after liberation one or both parents were found to be alive, these would often entrust the children to Zionist organizations believing that the young would receive permission to enter Palestine sooner than the old. They hoped to meet up with their offspring there.[424]

Helen Steiger is interviewing the Russian orphan Lene Walekirow while Walter Hahn (left) and Pjotre Fabiszewski are listening.

In February 1946 a group of forty Youth Aliyah[425] Hungarian Jews were housed in Indersdorf. Itzchak Gilboa, one of their group leaders, describes his background and the situation: "I was born in Hungary as Grünwald Endre. I survived with false papers the war. With a false name I left Hungary to the Russian Zone in Austria. With false papers I passed to the British Zone. Again with false papers I sneaked into the American Zone. I was leading a small group of children younger than me. We were members of

Dror Habonim. From Munich we traveled by train to Indersdorf to join a group of Hungarian Dror Habonim members. Our group became a strong unit."[426] The arrival of these Dror Habonim members marked the beginning of significant changes in the Children's Center: these refugees formed a unit of their own, considered their group to be a "kibbutz," and named it "Mahapechah."[427] They shared the same aims and ideas, and here above all, they expected to learn how to farm in order to acclimatize as quickly as possible to kibbutz life in the soon-to-be-founded state of Israel. Proudly, they wanted to stand on their own two feet and take charge of their group. The only thing they expected from the Children's Center was the best possible basic care. They kept apart from other residents and even staged a one-day strike for their autonomy.[428] They spent mornings working on the convent's farm and in the afternoons received instruction from their own Jewish-Hungarian teachers while at night they slept in rooms reserved for them alone. Zahava Szász Stessel recollects: "We learned Hebrew and general studies taught by educators (madrichim) from Eretz-Yisrael who joined our group. In the evenings we took long beautiful walks in the greenery around the fields. We kept busy watching sports tournaments and cheering the players, members of our group."[429]

Greta Fischer was most impressed by their discipline, their solidarity and their particular "social and political motivation." She noted that "the Zionists were most concerned with promoting good habits and keeping up morale. They prohibited lying, stealing and smoking or at least they tried to. They also wanted physical fitness training but by means of folk dancing, games and handicrafts. Most important, though, was education."[430] According to Fischer, Zionist groups encouraged living in collectives and in educating their group leaders to adhere to a strict code of ethics. The Sisters of Mercy also noted the exceptional role played by the kibbutz youngsters in Indersdorf, for members were "always calm and well behaved in the home" although they also showed little concern for the general welfare of the center. For instance, the gardener suddenly found that all the cucumbers had been harvested. "The Jewish helpers had jumped the gun on compensation for their work."[431] Moshe Ganan, one of the Kibbutz members, today has vivid memories of collecting potatoes in the fields or staying in the courtyard where the horses and stalls were. He was especially amazed about the nuns and their "cubicles at the end of the corridors, whence they could clandestinely watch the prayers and general worship going on in the church."[432] "Our first discovery — which later we were forbidden to repeat — was roaming the nearby path, plucking apples from the trees. It seems we were as yet a bit hungry — at least for fruits not served in an orderly way in the ghettos where we had lived only a year or so ago,"[433] he adds with a wry sense of humor.

"We were a great bunch," says Itzchak Gilboa (Endre Grünwald) today about his Hungarian Kibbutz group "Mahapechah." Moshe Ganan was among them and the sisters Katalin Szász (Zahava Stessel) and Erzsébet Szász (Hava Ginsburg).

Although several members of this Kibbutz group, like the sisters Katalin and Erzsébet Szász[434], were survivors of concentration camps and most of them orphans, their life was quite different from that of the others. Moshe Ganan is close to his post-war inner world, "From time to time I dreamed of my dead, killed mother and father, but we had our company replacing family life." He is sure that his group "never put on psychodramatic acts" of their recent past. They performed plays like *Jeremias* by

Stephan Zweig and Edgar Allan Poe's *The House of Usher* and *The Pit and the Pendulum*, dramatized by one of the members. They also held poetry-reading evenings, or sang together on the eves of Shabbath. Zionist songs were resounded "in general collective meetings just for the fun of it, but with time got quite fed up with it," he explains. "We did not hold sessions telling each other the ways we reached Germany or anything — a very natural inclination not to remember and not to revive recent horror stories."[435]

The group's solidarity posed an additional challenge on all the community when two members were diagnosed with tuberculosis. Because the administration was unable to quarantine them and even their Madrich couldn't control them, the two were taken against their will to the DP hospital in Gauting. For the three weeks of their stay at the Children's Center, they could easily have infected all the residents.[436]

Finally, this Hungarian kibbutz gained a considerable degree of autonomy when the International D.P. Children's Center Kloster Indersdorf moved to Prien on Chiemsee in July/August 1946, and the old cloister became a purely Jewish children's center under administration by the UNRRA and later the IRO.[437]

Attempting to plan for the future

What the future held in store was a burning and not easily answered question, especially for the Jewish youth. They couldn't and most didn't want to return to their homelands; they certainly didn't want to stay in the persecutors' country. But where should they go?

Shortly before destruction of the NS regime, governments and charitable organizations from nations as diverse as England, Norway, Australia, the USA and Switzerland let the US administration in Germany know that they were willing to adopt several hundred Jewish orphans. The suggestion, however, was vehemently denounced by representatives of Jewish survivors, the board of liberated Jews. They resolved that "not a single Jewish child, no matter what, will be sent anywhere other than directly to his or her only possible home, Eretz Israel."[438] UNRRA Team

182, however, proved indifferent to Jewish representatives' demands in Bavaria who wanted the few surviving Jewish children to be sent to Palestine. Staff made it possible, however, for representatives of Jewish organizations to promote emigration to Palestine, just as national liaison officers in the cloister could promote repatriation for their nationals. The team had a pluralistic and pragmatic orientation. That is, any solution was good as long as the survivor wanted it.

When the first group of 50 children left for England, these Jewish youths stayed behind, among them Szlama Weichselblatt, Miklos Roth, Jakub Kerker, Iwan Kisz, Abram Leder, Naftali Steinberg, Simcha Weiss, Morris Zeigelstein, Henryk Weinberg, Genia Edlermann, and the brothers Niedermann, Hahn, Farkas, Kniker.

Whereas many camp survivors expressed only vague desires — "Anywhere is fine as long as I can live in peace"[439] — the boys and girls in the kibbutz group imagined working together to build the state of Israel despite the fact that, in Palestine, tranquility could hardly be expected at that time. Others hoped for improved lifestyles and an opportunity for education and work in Western countries.[440] The UNRRA Team 182 couldn't make choices for the older children and teens but merely help them to find solutions in line with their desires. When, for instance, Nehemia Edlermann was given the option of going to Palestine but his sister Genia had not received her papers yet, Greta Fischer advised the two how to proceed. Genia let her brother go first, comforting herself with the thought that she would follow. But his letters described such a hard life, warning her not to come, that she decided to wait for the option to settle somewhere in the West.⁴⁴¹

If before the war, families had had plans to emigrate to certain countries, survivors oriented themselves accordingly. Greta Fischer used personal contacts in London to locate the sister of fifteen-year-old Czech Andrey Fried and thus facilitated his emigration. Other survivors, too, remembered relatives who had succeeded in fleeing before the war and who would be glad to help them now.⁴⁴²

Jakob Bulwa (back row left) and Sacher Israeler (front, on a soldier's lap) with their American liberators in Nabburg/Oberpfalz before arriving in Indersdorf.

When Sacher Israeler, the Farkas brothers or Milkos Roth wanted to live with their relatives in the USA, UNRRA Team 182 did everything possible to achieve this goal.⁴⁴³ In such cases, the first thing to do was find the relative's address and to procure written proof that the person would vouch for the young survivor. Then it could take months, if not years, before the USA or Canada provided a visa so that the child could really begin the journey.

Survivors needed a general statement of willingness from other nations to accept them, but for a while the world remained closed to them: Great Britain, the USA, Canada and Australia did not loosen their strict immigration policies until the end of the decade.

Michael desperately wanted to immigrate to the United States, but his wish couldn't be fulfilled. Naftali was sick and couldn't depart for England. In 1946 he joined his life-long friend Abram Leder for Palestine. Today he lives in Brazil.

Many of the older youths hoped to go to the USA, to the "America of their American soldiers."[444] When liberated they had enjoyed first aid as well as sympathetic and generous support from the American army. US soldiers had cultivated friendly relations with a number of the young DPs and had expressed interest in adopting certain individuals. The liberators conveyed the idea that the USA was a land of "milk and honey." As Greta Fischer wrote, "In the first flush of excitement and joy of liberation, many of the army personnel made commitments they were not able to fulfill, particularly in regard to taking children home with them or sending for them later, offering adoption, etc. From a psychological point of view, however, the effect of having first association after liberation with people who were interested in [them] and concerned about [their] welfare was salubrious."[445] In the first few months after the war ended, many of the boys had found temporary shelter with their American liberators and worked in the mess halls or barracks of individual army units. "Many came to the UNRRA DP centers and left the military units only because they found in the centers the best or only opportunity to search for relatives, to return home or to settle elsewhere."[446]

One example of this attachment is the Gentile Ukrainian boy Michael (Mike) Kolesnik. He was deported as a twelve-year-old orphan from Ukraine to Germany for forced labor. After liberation he was "adopted" by an American soldier. Mike insisted at first that he had absolutely no interest in returning to Eastern Europe and that he wanted only to wait for orders from his "sergeant."[447] As Greta Fischer noted: After six months of residence in the center Mike's enthusiasm about America has not dimmed, although he is less confident that his sergeant will send for him. ... He has real potentialities but cannot settle down to studying seriously or to prepar[ing] for a vocation because he is not sure of his future. This kind of situation is one of the most difficult in attempting to give the children a sense of security. They must know not only that they are wanted for the moment but also that someone is really planning for their future.[448] Youth like Mike needed devoted guidance to help uncover their talents and dreams and to find a new home that would truly welcome them.

After the group of fifty Jewish survivors had set out for England on October 31, 1945, those remaining at Indersdorf were generally hopeful and positive; however, as the next transportation option was slow to materialize, the delay had a demotivating effect on everyone left behind who now felt their options had shrunk. In January 1946 the mood reached its nadir: "Those not sent away became increasingly demoralized. In the beginning, when they believed another transport would soon be organized, they behaved in a praiseworthy way and made constructive contributions to life at the center. But as the weeks passed, they became more and more restless. Life in the Children's Center, although preferable by far [in comparison] to adult DP camps, had gradually become sterile and boring."[449] Staff observed a clear increase in anti-social behavior, tardiness to events, fights and theft, "a deceleration of rehabilitation."[450] To support her passionate plea for opening Western countries, Greta Fischer felt that at this point, the basic cause for so many of the undesirable behaviors could "not be treated in Germany."[451] Even if, by January 1946, the Children's Center was still a "young institution in the field of childcare," it was already "very old in the minds of those youngsters who had hoped that their sojourn at the center would be short, merely a necessary processing step before moving on – homeward or to new lands."[452] The search for relatives was, however, not yet over. "Much more intensive work must be done in this field." But the older ones were impatient, no longer willing to just waste time but instead itching to get a real new start somewhere else. Fischer understood that these youth needed an aim, and that their daily lives would have to unfold with this aim in mind.[453] Like all people, the young DPs wanted orientation, awareness of individual abilities, and some glimpse of what their days might mean before they could take the next steps in their return to life.

Of all those who had resided at Indersdorf, until July 1946 only 99 Jewish youths had emigrated from Germany. With help from the AJJDC, on April 9, 1946, twenty-eight young people left the center for Palestine; on the same day thirteen young Jews and on April 27 another seven left for the USA. In this period, four young Czechs also returned to their homeland.[454]

Abram Leder, Naftali Steinberg and Halina Bryks belonged to the aforementioned group of twenty-eight Jewish youth who insisted on going to Israel and succeeded in doing so.[455] Abram Leder's description shows the DPs' individual choice: "They [the UNRRA staff] asked each of us where we wanted to go, whether to our country of origin or to America; but all the Jews (of our group) wanted to go to Eretz Israel, which at that time was called Palestine," he wrote in his memoirs. British authorities permitted them to leave the country in April 1946.[456] Leder described the trip and the new start enjoyed by the young survivors in Palestine: "They [the UNRRA] brought us to the port of Marseille in France; we boarded the Champollion and sailed to Eretz Israel. After three days at sea, we reached the port of Haifa in Eretz Israel. The country was ruled by the British at that time. We were quarantined for a few days, and then the Jewish Agency[457] sent all of us, me and my friend Naftali included, to a *moschav*[458] called Kfar Hittim near Tiberias. We worked for half a day and studied for half a day."[459] In this way, the road to the young survivor's dream of a new home was paved.

Young survivors studying agriculture in Palestine. (Halina Bryks (Chana Porat) 2nd from right in 2nd row).

Miklos Roth was received by his aunt in New York in 1946; Bernat Zelikovits found two uncles in Canada and was finally permitted to join them in Toronto. Roman and Leon Kniker, Jakob Kerker, Iwan Kisz and Jakob Bulwa managed later to reach their dreamland America. Isolated in families that had no idea of what these youngsters had just been through, they stuck it out under much harder conditions than the English "Boys"[460] who stayed together for a while in different hostels in England.[461]

Repatriating Gentile children and teenagers

As with adult DPs, children and youths from Western Europe were relatively quickly repatriated to their respective countries; for instance, the last French transport with eight little children left Indersdorf in the first week of July 1946; among the group were around 15 bigger kids up to twelve years old and four Belgian children who had not been accepted by Belgium.[462]

The first group of girls from Upper Silesia were repatriated together with other Polish children in June 1946 (among them Angela Gogolin, Maria Knet, Regina Cierpiol, Ursula Goretzki).

Gradually, many of the Eastern Europeans returned to their homelands, as did, for instance, in June 1946 about 100 adult DPs and 111 girls and boys from various DP camps including Kloster Indersdorf. Accompanying them on the train was UNRRA staff member Edna Davis who reported a good mood, Polish songs and flags, luxurious meals and the young people's willingness to care for the babies and keep the cabins clean.[463] Due to a misunderstanding the children could not, as planned, be given over to their relatives at the station in Katowice but had to spend a few days in a transit children's home about fifty kilometers away in Kozle. A few days later, those who still had parents were picked up there;

but as the Polish orphans also reacted positively to their Polish caregivers, Edna Davis's subsequent glowing report persuaded 27 other youths to return. Thus, in mid-July 1946, many long-term Gentile Polish residents of Kloster Indersdorf could be repatriated.[464]

With drawing, singing and needle work the girls are spending the exciting time of their journey home.

But there were other Gentile children whose situation was desperate, as Lillian D. Robbins noted in September 1947: "However, there are other children who [have been] rejected by their own national officers or who, because of previous experiences, reject for themselves the opportunity to return. The former ... are truly outcasts. ... [But] they, too, plead for a chance to start life anew, to settle down, to live in peace."[465] "These children want to capture some of the years they have lost. Many of them have dreamed and planned for years to emigrate to a country that can offer educational and economic opportunities. Surely they deserve a chance to do so as many of your forebears have done before you," Lillian D. Robbins, former director of the Indersdorf

Children's Center, told her American audience. This was especially true for many of the Eastern Europeans, especially citizens of the Soviet Union. They feared reprisals, or they rejected the new political system. In Kloster Indersdorf there were also more than a few young people who refused at first to be repatriated. The national liaison officers from these countries who visited the center were equally disinclined to persuade them otherwise.[466] In consequence, one Soviet liaison officer accused the UNRRA team of teaching "anti-Soviet propaganda." Team 182 felt that in such cases it was best to stick to soft, patient efforts at persuasion; yet "in a few instances, children themselves preferred continued separation from their parents. This was due, in some cases, to unwillingness to return to countries of origin, as with followers of King Peter of Yugoslavia and members of the Polish Scout movement."[467]

Although they were expected to show political neutrality, it was probably in part due to the UNRRA staff's attempts to delay unwanted repatriation that only at the end of 1946 while the center itself had been moved to Prien on Chiemsee, thirty-eight Soviet children could be transported back to the Soviet Union. Greta Fischer, an UNRRA doctor and a nurse accompanied the group to Gutenfürst, southwest of Plauen, a train station on the border of the Soviet Zone from where they would travel further via Frankfurt on the Oder into Russia accompanied by ten nurses and a physician. There the children would be housed in orphanages or with foster parents or relatives. When leaving Germany, many of the children, especially the older ones, were visited by sad memories. Valentina Fedorina, for instance, remembered being brought as a forced laborer together with her parents to Germany where in Heilbronn she had lost sight of them. She had worked hard in a factory and on a farm. In the meantime she had learned of her mother's death and of her father's simply having disappeared without a trace. As she sat in the train, she sighed, "I came with my father and mother to Germany. I go from Germany alone."[468]

Moving the International D.P. Children's Center from Kloster Indersdorf to Prien on Chiemsee

These young people – Jewish and Gentile – constantly experienced "the rug being pulled out from under their feet." Greta Fischer felt their longing for the security of a permanent home. As for provisional solutions such as transfer in groups from one institution to another or moving the Children's Center to a different location, she found them neither wholesome nor to be recommended: "Movement that requires readjustment but does not lead to a final answer may be less satisfactory than no movement at all."[469]

The teens needed stability and security in their lives, and their caregivers, too, had to be protected from constant changes and interruptions as well as the continual challenge, really too great, of having to empathize with each wave of new arrivals. Nonetheless, the demand for improved quarters was decisive, given conditions during the long winter of 1945/46 and especially during the fortnight of diphtheria-related quarantine when everything had to take place within the convent's walls. This desire for improvement was taken seriously by the headquarters of the UNRRA. On February 19, 1946, the UNRRA had reached an agreement with the US military that permitted expansion of their areas of responsibility and authority. The organization was now dedicated to replacing mixed-nationality assembly centers with religious and, for the most part, nationally homogeneous ones where DPs would live together in larger units to enable more effective care and a broader spectrum of educational and training options.

The second director of the Indersdorf Children's Center, Jean Margaret Henshaw, had taken a trip through Germany that included the Chiemsee. She liked the picturesque region much better than Indersdorf. Therefore she tried to convince the military to take possession of the biggest hotels and mansions in Prien and the surrounding area. She saw to it that most of the still resident children and youth in Indersdorf, including foreign personnel at the end of July and beginning of August 1946, moved to the Chiemsee.[470]

Greta Fischer was against the move. But after the death of six children,[471] she also hoped to find on the Chiemsee a more beautiful site as well as a more healthful climate.[472] Another reason to move was that in this popular vacation spot, the largest hotels — six major buildings — were available for housing separated according to age, religion, and nationality. The team had struggled through to see this as a good opportunity: "We could give much better individual attention. We had houses for babies, ... houses for toddlers, and ... houses for the big children [now]."[473] Hotel Kronprinz became the administration building for these UNRRA children's homes; at the same time the building served the children, ill, small and in special need of care, as well as quarantined new arrivals or youth with contagious diseases.[474] The luxurious Strand Hotel, with a dock for boats, could also easily be isolated from the German community.[475] Here up to 150 Orthodox Jews from Hungarian and Romanian-speaking areas were supposed to live together and enjoy a kosher kitchen.[476]

Zoltán Farkas (2nd from right) with friends in a rowboat in front of Strand Hotel (today Yacht Hotel) in Prien on Chiemsee (1946).

The somewhat smaller Seehotel was reserved for Jewish youth from Poland and Czechoslovakia. It was now possible to set up houses for different age-groups: the four to twelve-year-old Jewish and Gentile children were to be cared for in the Hotel Kampenwand; the Hotel Chiemsee was reserved for up to 110 exclusively Gentile youths. In Gstadt, nine kilometers away, three houses had been requisitioned for 85 little children under four while the Posthotel in Prien would serve as a warehouse.[477]

A completely new team of volunteers in Indersdorf maintained the name "Team 182" while the old team members now on the Chiemsee joined groups variously called team 188, 634 and 1069. Greta Fischer became the director of the "International D.P. Children's Center Hotel Kronprinz" in Prien.

Young people with their chaperones from UNNRA Team 188 in Prien (Harry C. Parker with the pipe, Genia Edlermann in the back row, 2nd from left).

Before the move, Kloster Indersdorf housed (still or once again) 250 young people and 76 small children. The older girls and boys moved from Indersdorf to Prien at the end of July 1946 while the toddlers' transfer took a little longer because the dormitories had not yet been completely furnished. The Sisters took care of those left behind[478] until finally the day came: "On August 9 the last of the tiniest children were driven off in an ambulance and on August 10 the last six sick children were picked up."[479] When they moved, the UNRRA team from Indersdorf took their inventory with them, including children's beds, laundry, kitchen utensils, chickens and even a number of recently slaughtered pigs. With the children foremost in mind plus the unfurnished houses not yet suitable for residence, Greta Fischer even successfully fought for Indersdorf director Jean Margaret Henshaw's agreement to take along some things that belonged to the convent.[480]

The first few days after moving in, the staff was enthusiastic about the beautiful mansions and charming landscape directly on the Chiemsee. Only a few months later, the noble Strandhotel would already house 160 young people from 16 to 18 years old, mainly Jewish refugees from Hungary, Poland, Romania and Czechoslovakia. A kosher kitchen was installed, the isolated location guarded against conflict between German and Jewish youth better than before. But because at first neither lessons nor sports were offered, the boys and girls were very bored and tended to remain in bed until noon. On October 1, 1946, the Dutch director Hendrika Walvis complained to the UNRRA authorities about the unacceptable conditions in her institution and asked urgently for help.[481] A while later, an ORT school offered useful courses in welding, auto mechanics, tailoring and photography.[482]

In Prien the staff confronted well-known as well as unknown problems: paths between the various buildings were long; there were not enough teachers and staff; there was too little furniture, clothing, nourishing food, medicines, hygienic articles and light bulbs. A ruling that DPs were to be given job preference over Germans meant that the Sisters of Mercy were not brought along to Prien. The UNRRA staff, however, missed their help, above all, when it came to caring for infants and in general house-management. "It was hardest to do without the Sisters. Miss Fischerova remonstrated but her request was denied. The UNRRA was determined to hire mostly foreigners to give them work so that they wouldn't simply rely on UNRRA to take good care of them,"[483] as the Sisters saw it.

To keep fluctuation down, the various UNRRA teams on the Chiemsee tried to take in only long-term residents. They could come from DP camps or DP communities and included all ages.

Staff saw their main task in searching for relatives and reorienting their clients toward "earlier cultural patterns." Children under 16 were generally viewed as "able to be repatriated," with the exception of Jews, Ukrainians and youth from the Balkans.[484] Jewish youngsters could only be accepted if they proved they had been in the US Zone since December 21, 1945.[485]

Nonetheless, even in Prien the young people had to wait to be sent on, and therefore 400 foreign children and young adults continued to be housed in facilities on the Chiemsee; half of them were Jewish, and, until 1947, the various UNRRA teams tried to find solutions for them. Those who wanted to go to Palestine were often successful, and against the will of the British, were smuggled in by Jewish aid organizations. This act of daring was more easily carried out from the American than from the British Zone because the British governing the Mandate wanted to keep the number of Jewish refugees entering Palestine down to an absolute minimum.[486]

The possibilities for legal emigration to the UK or the USA remained limited. The earlier Indersdorf UNRRA director Lillian D. Robbins gave a passionate speech at the annual conference of the American National Federation of Settlements in which she begged America to finally offer these uprooted children a secure home: "While nations are negotiating new borders, reparations and economic advantages, the unaccompanied displaced United Nations' child in Germany under the protection of the United Nations is losing weeks, months, possibly even years that can never be regained. That child knows the result of exploitation, of national greed, of war. He can grow up [to become] a bitter, disillusioned, selfish adult, interested only in what works to his own advantage. But such a child can also become the most important contributor to building a new world, where international cooperation is the cornerstone. The United Nations have responsibility for paving the way. Which path should it be?"[487] To convince the delegates, she told Kurt Klappholz's story. Having been granted a visa to England, he had been admitted to the London School of Economics: "And there are many other Kurts still in Germany, a great many, who are wasting their time in DP camps because they have no place to go."[488] It is possible that the world's aversion to accepting the young survivors stemmed from inability or unwillingness to believe what had happened in Europe under the Nazis. As Greta Fischer experienced first-hand, "Part of my family were in London. And the first time I went to London, I was telling my friends, my family all the things that I had seen. And nobody wanted to believe the stories. I mean, my family believed me – but friends said, 'It can't be! It can't be that human beings can do this thing to other human beings! It is impossible!'"[489]

For the young people, the situation was intolerable. They would say, "It was terrible that we lost our homes; it was terrible that we lost our parents; but the worst thing is, we have no country, we are stateless and nobody really knows about us and nobody wants us."[490] For some, the waiting just became too long, which led to attacks against Germans and to looting: "[The young people] were very aggressive, sure. The children were very hostile to their environment and we always felt very sorry."[491] Nonetheless, Greta Fischer was able to see something positive in the need to wait: "… it seemed to make the children more secure when the next step was ahead of them."[492] The staff tried to "use the time in a constructive way to deal with the many symptoms of antisocial behavior which could not have been corrected if there had been no time to build up deeper, more meaningful relationships and to get to know the youngsters more intimately and not only their distrustful façade."[493]

In the end, Eugenius Kamer immigrated to Cuba to live with his aunt, uncle and cousin. Genia Edlermann (Jean Sugar) was permitted to go to Canada, while Zoltán and Erwin Farkas could join their relatives in the USA.

For a large number of survivors, prospects opened at the end of 1947 when Canada declared its willingness to take 1,000 young Jewish refugees.[494] And "some of those children did [indeed go] to Canada. The offer came in '47 and [with it] a request for a social worker who had worked in Germany to come to Canada [as well] to help with … integration." This signaled for Greta Fischer the end of her employment with the UNRRA: "I was very attached to those children, very attached [and] so I applied for the job."[495] Truly concerned to see how things would go for them, she accompanied a group of Jewish youth to Canada and was responsible for the integration of another group of young survivors into Canadian society.

The Jewish Children's Center Kloster Indersdorf, August 1946 to September 1948

After the International D.P. Children's Center moved from Indersdorf to Prien, only the Hungarian kibbutz group remained behind. "We were the only inhabitants in the cloister, some 40 kids, getting forged as a cohesive company, waiting for certificates? — No, not really, waiting for the time the Zionist movement would find an opening to pack us on a car and take us to Erez Israel, our homeland,"[496] Moshe Ganan describes this situation. "We lived there, in the cloister, without emerging from it. American soldiers stood at the entrance, throwing away fat cigarette-butts which the poor Germans were collecting as valuables. We were bewildered, strange foreign place, no permit to roam the vicinity."[497] In the old convent's building, with a wholly new UNRRA Team 182, an exclusively Jewish children's home for young refugees from Central and Eastern Europe was created.[498]

Polish Kibbutz group at the entrance to the Jewish Children's Center Kloster Indersdorf (1947).

The new team was not blessed with an easy start because many of the things urgently needed in a children's center had been taken away to Prien.[499] But in the end Jewish organizations like the AJJDC, Dror[500] or other Jewish agencies sent material and staff assistance.

The Polish Kibbutz group dancing the Hora in front of the Kloster Indersdorf brewery.

After the first month in service, in September 1946, the new director M. D'Aloja could already report 363 residents, among them were 85 adult DPs, one doctor, four teachers and two cooks to help with the work. The new team set up a kindergarten, a primary and a middle school. Languages of instruction were Yiddish and Hebrew. Excursions were taken to Munich's zoo and puppet theatre; movies in Dachau were also enjoyed. On Jewish holidays, theater groups sprang into action. The social work department continued to suffer under a dearth of personnel and longed to have a trained psychologist on staff. In mid-September 1946, "like a breath of fresh air," Shulamit Katz "magically materialized" — conjured up from Palestine by the Jewish Agency to facilitate emigration to Eretz Israel.[501] Katz recalled the desolate situation she found on arrival but, as representative of the Promised

Land, took things in hand within the first few days because the children were highly motivated to do anything to qualify for Aliyah – emigration.[502] "To open the school we had 100 notebooks and pencils. We tore pages out of the notebooks, cut the pencils in half and gave them to the pupils."[503] And at first their "eyes twinkled with enthusiasm"; later, however, their interest in school waned somewhat.

In the fall of 1946, about two-thirds of the residents were Polish and another third Hungarian.[504] These national groups lived on different floors in the building and were hindered in communication by the language barrier. A secret radio station that had been set up in a small room kept direct contact with the liberation movement in Palestine.[505] In November 1946 the Children's Center census still recorded 361 residents, including 141 boys and 112 girls.[506] In December these figures were 344 residents, including 123 boys and 108 girls although within a single month 37 young people from other camps arrived while 61 from Indersdorf were transferred to Ansbach and Rosenheim or into hospitals.[507] Then, in the winter of 1946-47, suddenly "two hundred children arrived," among them many who "had come to Bavaria without clothing or shoes."[508] The original Hungarian kibbutz group left for Leipheim. Moshe Ganan paints a vivid picture of the group's journey to Palestine: "Then one day we were — shortly prepared — invited to ascend cars, I presume the big studebaker-cars, and we were gone, to Munich (blasted glass ceiling, only holes, nothing whole) and off to France, through Lyon, to Cayolle, Salon, Marseille. We were traveling Holocaust-type, i. e. not exactly sleeping cars and couchettes, but bare wagons, but we did not mind, not much comfort, but we managed. A month or so we were there. Once again it was winter, 1946 turning 1947. Then we were taken in well-closed cars through southern France — some said we traveled round and round in order that nobody may follow us and know our whereabouts. In the end we alighted on a sea-shore, whence I could see a small ship which would, I presumed, take us to the real ship that would take us to Eretz Israel. But the ship did not take us to any other ship, it was the old leaky tub going taking some 600 emigrants, young, old, men and women through the straits of Messina to the shores of Greece and Israel. We ate very hard cakes and drank raw lemons. Some trusted sailors were given money to buy us food on the shore, but they lost their bearings and never returned to the ship. The ship leaked and we, I too, worked hours on the pumps to get loose of the overdraft of water. We slept on 40 cm X some 1.80 meter long bunks. Many being sea-sick. I was not sea-sick and was very proud of the fact. I also found a fountain-pen falling on me from a higher echelon, so I was kept happy by it for the long – more than a month – way. Only after the British ships caught us and conquered our tub and transferred us to their famous warships Ocean Vigour and Empire Royal taking us to Cyprus fell my spirit – I sewed my parent's picture into the cover of a canvass-bound notebook I had and the English took it from me. Now for the first time I felt bereaved and ... wept."[509]

Later the majority of those who found shelter in Kloster Indersdorf would be Hungarian Dror Zionist youth who spoke no Yiddish. A special event was the European-wide meeting of the Dror movement in Indersdorf around Passover in spring 1947. Dror leader Yitzhak Tabenkin opened the ceremonies that included folk dances, recitation of poems, theater performances and Jewish songs. The children showed their enthusiasm for the Kibbutz movement.[510]

Some of the smallest inhabitants of Kloster Indersdorf were among the 400 orphans who appeared as extras in the partial documentary "The Search," directed by Hollywood's Fred Zinnemann.[511] The film illustrates the "typical" fate of these uprooted children in the postwar era.[512]

The Jewish children's center lived on for two more years in Indersdorf with an average of between 200 and 350 young residents: "Sometimes there was ample room and at others we had to squeeze in because more had come but few had departed for the Promised Land and left the cloister."[513] When larger groups departed, the empty places would soon be filled: via Austria throughout 1947, Zionist youth organizations brought more Jewish orphans from Eastern Europe, especially Romania, to the German DP camps.[514] A staff member of Youth Aliyah reported: "The installations in Bayerisch Gmain and Indersdorf filled up again ...; children arrived nearly naked and hungry."[515] Many children and youth from the transit DP camp Rosenheim took refuge after its closing in Indersdorf.[516]

Interior of the Kloster Indersdorf chapel after the last residents had left. For three years the room had been used for concerts, theater and other events.

Altogether it is estimated that, between 1945 and 1948, Kloster Indersdorf sheltered more than 1,000 children and young people. The residents of the "Jewish Children's Center Kloster Indersdorf" found new homes primarily in the Kibbutzim Beit Hashita, Netiv HaLamed-hei, Ein Harod, Tel Josef, Hefzi-Ba, Na'an and Ashdot-Jaakov.[517] After the State of Israel was founded, the Jewish children's center was disbanded in September 1948.[518] The last to leave demolished the interior of this old Bavarian convent building.

Learning to Live with the Aftermath

The Allied psychologists' expert group defined three criteria for successful adult repatriation. First, the victim must have recovered physically and have returned to a responsible place within the family and the community. The individual must also have passed through a process of mourning; that is, to have overcome a phase of regression, social withdrawal, and selfishness to end by being "less selfish and more altruistic," the sign of recovery from "serious emotional losses" and of renewed ability to "integrate on an adult level."[519] Third, the expert group rewarded the triumph over "feelings of unreality, restlessness, apathy or irritability."[520] Given these criteria, we can only guess how much more difficult a successful rehabilitation would be for children and youth who could not be repatriated and had to recreate their lives in entirely new surroundings.

"If the Americans[521] succeed in making half-way normal people out of the 250 orphans and foundlings, children of foreign slave laborers who are in the care of the UNRRA at Kloster Indersdorf, they will have performed a miracle,"[522] the *Süddeutsche Zeitung* concluded in December 1945. "Kloster Indersdorf is merely a transit stop. Once the children have grown stronger physically and mentally, they are sent back to their supposed homelands to restart their lives."[523] Most young bodies luckily recover very quickly; whether this is true of young souls can only be answered subjectively by the individuals involved. The UNRRA Team 182 did its best, however, to create a therapeutic environment in which rehabilitation could commence. In Kloster Indersdorf and later in Prien, the displaced children were offered the finest care possible. And the uprooted youngsters did recover surprisingly quickly, their improved health surely a function of adequate nourishment, medical attention and all-around quality nurturing. What took place, as in other venues too, was considered "a wonder." In less than a month, you could see "how the children got used to a well-regulated school day with its organized games and routines, together with friends of the same background and hopes for the future. Their faces, after only a few weeks, regained their glow; they began to sound like carefree children singing and talking. You could tell just by looking at them and checking the medical records that they had begun to gain weight and grow taller," United Nations staff member Norwegian Mathilde Oftedal reported to a US Senate Committee in Washington in 1947.[524]

The young Jewish survivors Hans Neumann (middle), Julius Weiss and Wolf Witelson became sailors (1947).

In the first international Children's Center in the American Zone, stable living conditions and proper care brought positive change. Greta Fischer felt this was due "in large part to the relative degree of physical comfort, plenty of food, clean sheets, suitable clothing with some choice among the children."[525] Their physical recovery had a positive effect on their spirits. It was also important, however, that the young survivors of so many destructive experiences received empathy, individual attention and the feeling of being valued. Even though the losses and trauma could not be reversed, proper nurture could bolster a sense of self-worth and contribute to emotional healing, especially if the children were enabled to feel at liberty within the given circumstances and make their own decisions. At the same time, in an intimate personal relationship between child and mentor lay the cornerstone for successful behavior modification. UNRRA Team 182 also exhibited its expertise with their empathic awareness of the young survivors' spiritual and emotional potential whose development they encouraged as best they could. An expression of this is Greta Fischer's lifelong admiration for the young people's "indomitable spirit," their "will to survive," and their "indescribable rage to live ... which transcended the terrible hardship they had been made to endure." She saw in their hopes a sign of spiritual triumph and the "living proof that the human spirit is indestructible."[526] Greta Fischer and her colleagues felt that the smallest children would make up for developmental delays. They hoped that the teenagers' courage and desire would help them to deal with the effects of their trauma and enable them to forge meaningful lives. The UNRRA staff understood what the children most urgently needed immediately after liberation and took great pains to fulfill these longings to develop individual talents and abilities. Thirty-six years later Greta Fischer evaluated this achievement: "In Kloster Indersdorf the children found physical health and the beginning of a moral and spiritual rehabilitation."[527]

And How Life Went On …

Of course, we want to know how the "moral and spiritual rehabilitation" of these children and teens worked out, whether and how they were able to master their lives.[528] Therese Divak, Alexander Pecha, Lene Walekirow, Michael Kolesnik, Sofie Rybki and many others who returned to Poland or nations belonging to the former Soviet Union have not yet been found. But fortunately, some of the displaced girls from Upper Silesia have been rediscovered in Poland, and 50 of the Jewish youths have been traced to the four corners of the globe; a succession of them have returned to "their" Kloster Indersdorf to talk about their experiences with school classes and the local people as well as to share recollections and follow up on friendships. Those who were small children then but have now entered retirement have come back from France, for instance, to search for information about their parents and learn at least something more about their roots. Because they were too little to remember their stay at the convent, they come back thirsty for any little detail about their early lives. Walter Beausert, Daniel Mariewski (Baumann) and Gisela Magula (Gisèle Niango) call their desire for knowledge about their parents' motives "une rage de savoir" or "une rage de comprendre."[529]

The Polish children Zofia Karpuk (now Oglaza) and Janusz Karpuk talk about conditions in Polish orphanages and developments in their own professional and private lives. Both now have families of their own. Janusz played handball on Poland's national team; he also became a metal worker, sports trainer and wood carver. Zofia became a chemist in the textile industry. Janusz describes himself as someone who has always been a quiet man, closed in, who speaks little and has been prevented from enjoying intimate friendships because he is unable to express his feelings towards others.

Following a trauma such as losing their closest relatives, people who don't give up but instead develop those traits that enable them to go on are called "resilient." The children and youngsters of that time – at least those "rediscovered" – showed an astonishing resilience. They integrated into their new environments and seized opportunities as they came along. They learned trades that permitted them to earn a living and often to start families. They were able to manage the pressures of the working world, did not commit crimes, and psychologically did nothing to draw special attention to themselves.[530]

In 2008 Janusz visits the Bavarian farm where his mother died.

Greta Fischer herself could go on with her social work and help Jewish orphans to integrate into Canadian society. During the immediate years that followed and until her death in 1988, she observed that "despite the fears of governments" most of the child survivors "were able to establish normal lives wherever they went with some achieving distinguished careers."[531]

Even if it remains difficult to measure the extent of recovery, it is certainly relevant to ask whether the young survivors left Indersdorf to enter an environment that protected, understood, supported and encouraged them; whether they had the company of siblings or friends or whether they were totally alone in the world. Could they still draw on certain resources from their parental homes? When introducing Holocaust Memorial Day to the UN General Assembly on the 60th anniversary of the liberation of Auschwitz, success story Roman Kniker (Roman Kent) recalled his early childhood: "In my youth I learned what it meant to be part of a family. ... I learned that I existed because others cared for me, loved me. My life had value. The memory of my family, of the love I came to know and practice, helped me to survive the Holocaust. No matter what happened in the concentration camps, no matter what the Germans did to me, they could not succeed in convincing me that we did not matter and that our lives were not of value. I continued."[532] This helped him in the camps and later afforded him the necessary self-confidence. Roman Kniker succeeded in the classic manner "from rags to riches": he built up a major international retail business and has represented the interests of Jewish Holocaust survivors worldwide.[533]

Some of the Indersdorf "Boys" in England with their wives during a wedding. (3 couples starting 2nd from left: Charlotte + Salek Benedikt, Fay + Eric Hitter, Gwyneth + Kurt Klappholz. From right: Hettie + Alec Ward)

As time passed and they followed their pursuits in various countries, many youths lost the solidarity they had known at Indersdorf. Today they live in Israel, the USA, Belgium, Canada, Brazil and elsewhere. Only the "Boys" in England who still call themselves that and are members of the *Survivors '45 Aid Society* meet regularly in the Holocaust Survivors' Center in the northwest section of London. Avram Warszaw (Alec Ward), Salek Benedikt, Manfred Haymann (Heyman), Martin and Jakob (Jack) Hecht, and many others are still in close contact with one another.

Although they were under the aegis of Orthodox aid societies, whether they were sent to strictly religious or liberal institutions depended on the orientation of their parental homes and their own desires. Lazar (Leslie) Kleinmann for instance, kept his promise to God and accompanied Bernat (Dov) Nasch and the Hecht brothers to a Yeshiva in Manchester.

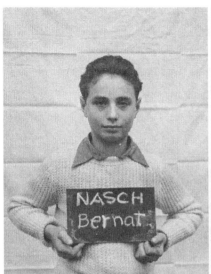

Today Bernat Nasch calls himself Dov and lives in Antwerp.

Most of the "Boys" succeeded in learning a trade and founding a family. Kurt Klappholz, for instance, quickly perfected his English and became a lecturer at the renowned London School of Economics.[534] At some point, while standing by the tower clock at Golders Green, it suddenly occurred to him that he had achieved the aim his father had longed to accomplish – leading his life in a Western democracy. When after ten promiscuous years he finally fell in love for the first time, a wave of strong feelings broke over him: guilt, mourning for a multitude of losses, and hatred for the murderers of his parents. At this time he sought psychotherapy. Eventually, he married a Welsh Gentile, Gwyneth, became the father of two sons and maintained a close friendship with Salek Benedikt until his death in 1999.

Salek Benedikt, going by the name of Benny Benedikt, became a successful graphic artist and now in his 80s continues to lay out the *Journal of the Holocaust Survivors '45 Aid Society*. His photographic memory permits exact recall of many details concerning the Indersdorf Children's Center, and it pains him still not to have been able to uncover the fate of his brother.

Manfred Haymann (Heyman) managed to see his ill mother in Sweden in 1947 before she died of tuberculosis. Every year he attends the memorial service in Flossenbürg to say Kaddish, the Jewish prayer for the dead, for his father Wilhelm and his brother Eugen. Abram Warszaw (Alec Ward), who became a ladies' tailor, is invited to give eyewitness testimony in schools and synagogues and with his beautiful voice always includes the Yiddish songs he sang in the ghetto while begging for bread for his family. He has never returned to Germany, convinced that his state of health would not permit it.

Jewish survivors with their pictures from Kloster Indersdorf. (2010 reunion, from left:) Mendel Tropper, Eric Hitter, Leslie Kleinman, Maier and Smuel Reinstein, Dov Nasch, Abram Leder and Martin Hecht.

Bernat (Dov) Nasch saw the world for a long time as though "through fog"; he had little interest in school and landed in Belgium via England and Israel – for the sake of love. Today his family and activity as a witness of those times are the center of his life. Almost daily he meets his dear friend from Indersdorf, Imre (Eric) Hitter, at the Diamond Bourse of Antwerp. He speaks many languages and serves as an interpreter for participants at the survivors' reunions; his memoirs have been published in Belgium.[535]

The survivors who went to Palestine often lived in Kibbutzim first, struggling hard to contribute to the founding of the State of Israel. Most members of the Hungarian Kibbutz "Mahapechah" found refuge in Kibbutz Hefci-ba. Moshe Ganan, one of them, reflects his time there: "They accepted us, new immigrants coming to Israel, but we never spoke of our recent past. It was a fact well-known but absolutely not cultivated. We were meant to be acculturated and turned into maybe "sabres," inborn, as fast as we could, a trend including forgetting our past and turning our back on it, somehow. We learned fast a new language, a new way of life, to which our Holocaust past was foreign, our culture strange and mostly unwelcome, as such. Filled with a new zeal for our much-yearned new land, we turned — to our utmost ability — our back on our unfaithful-to-us past and culture, trying to assimilate to the new one."[536] Today he lives in Jerusalem and has published twelve books of prose and poetry. He is in touch with his friends from "Mahapechah" Zahava Stessel in New York City and Itzchak Gilboa in Phoenix, Arizona.

Jadwiga Schulikowska, one of the babies of a Polish forced laborer, was adopted by a Polish couple. In the 1980s, as a wife and mother of three children, she finally had the chance to meet her birth mother again, but sadly, her birth father, who had wanted to find her, too, had long since passed away.[537]

Life afterwards has not always been as easy as many have hoped and expected. Tibor Munkácsy was already married when in 1950 he finally got the permission to move from the UK to his US-American dreamland. But at this time, the luck of his successful half-brother, the famous fashion photographer Martin Munkácsi, had dispersed. Martin could no longer help him to start a new life because he was sick and had lost all his money. Tibor himself had to struggle hard until he managed to work as a cameraman with celebreties like Jane Fonda, Jackie Kennedy, Jack

Nicholson or Marlon Brando. When he had to stand on New York's skyscrapers to take pictures for the Hollywood film industry, he thought, "If I have survived Buchenwald, I will survive this."[538]

Michael (Miklos) Roth at the 2008 Indersdorf reunion with Helen Patton (granddaughter of General George Patton, Jr).

Szlama Weichselblatt located his father in the USA, but this reunion was also quite a disappointment. Ira Wexler lived in poor conditions and was estranged from his son after being separated from him for eight years. Szlama changed his name to the more American-sounding Sol D. Wexler. In the 50s in New York he met his old friends from Indersdorf all together one more time — the Farkas brothers, Miklos Roth, Lillian D. Robbins and Helen Steiger – only to disappear afterward without a trace. During the reunions in Indersdorf other survivors continued to inquire, whether their friend "Wexler" was rediscovered. They had to wait until May 2012, when Sol D. Wexler was found again in New York, thanks to a caver who brought Weichselblatt's incredible story of survival in Ukranian caves to light.[539]

Zoltán and Erwin Farkas finally realized, as eighty-year-olds, that there never has been a moment in their lives when they were willing to admit that all of their large family perished in the Holocaust. In the USA they had carried on without the emotional and social support of parents, grandparents and siblings, always with a "subliminal sadness," as Zoltán, despite considerable professional success, described his state of mind.[540] When asked about his favorite song, he answers "Gloomy Sunday."[541] Despite the geographical distance, Lazar (Leslie) Kleinmann remained in touch with his childhood friends, the Farkas brothers. He married Evelyn, a Gentile German, earned his living as a manufacturer of ladies' coats and suits and has two children and a granddaughter. In his eighties, several years after Evelyn's death, he made up for the Bar Mitzvah he had missed at age thirteen. In England he married his second wife, Miriam, and he lives close to a synagogue where he goes to pray every morning. He is a popular speaker and ambassador for reconciliation, tolerance, and brotherly love.

Abram Leder from Israel with one of the Sisters of Mercy from Kloster Indersdorf in 2008.

Many of the former residents of Kloster Indersdorf have sadly passed away: Roman Weinstock, Hans Neumann, Miklos Roth, Julius Weiss, Mordecai Topel, Zdzislaw Szymanek, Martha Cierpiol, Fischel Kampel and many others. Kurt Klappholz is missed for his unique personal qualities and Eugenius Kamer's children remember their father's "incredible zest for life."[542]

During a visit in July 2008 Steve (Sacher) Israeler recognizes himself in a 1945 photo from Kloster Indersdorf.

Many survivors attend the reunions that have been held annually since 1995 at the Flossenbürg concentration camp memorial. Those who were cared for in the immediate postwar years in Kloster Indersdorf have been going there since 2008. Israeli survivors, for instance, have introduced their families first to the venue of their suffering and then in Indersdorf to the setting for their immediate postwar lives. They want their children and grandchildren to understand them and are surprised to discover to what extent the Germany they had known has altered. As Greta Fischer notes, they were all youngsters who had been sent away by desperate parents in order to save their lives, knowing that they themselves would not survive. These child survivors had been "abandoned, starved, humiliated, forced to beg, to steal food, having no shelter, beaten, sexually abused, degraded and routinely holding death with both hands. They had survived. Survived physically –

how? By chance? By their indomitable will to survive? Saved for something special? As a warning?"[543]

Until her death in 1988, Greta Fischer kept in touch with "her children" all over the world, continued to be amazed by their "indomitable" will to live, their "indescribable rage to live" and spirit of humanity – despite all their traumas. "Some of them want to forget their past. Some of them know they mustn't forget their past; some of them have never talked to their children. The last few years many of the second generation have had problems because there was some sort of secret in the family. ... The parents wanted to protect their children. This is very well meaning but [fails to understand that] the past must be remembered, that the past is part of your existence."[544] For her entire life, Greta Fischer insisted that survivors had a responsibility – to themselves and others – to talk about their experiences of the Holocaust. She believed to the end in the healing power of remembrance.

Greta Fischer – Stages in a Life

Greta Fischer was the sixth and last child of veterinarian Leopold Fischer and his wife Ida Fischerova, née Mayer, in Budišov in today's Czech Republic. Seventy-eight years later at a crowded Jerusalem bus station she would succumb to a fatal heart attack and be buried in Kibbutz Magen on the border of the Gaza Strip. To remind us of this remarkable woman, a simple engraved stone reads:
Greta Fischer, 19.1.1910 – 28.9.1988

Greta Fischer (right) and her older siblings Trude, Erna, Honza, Robert and Paul with their parents (photo from around 1915).

The Jewish Fischer family lived surrounded by German ethnics in Moravia; Greta spoke German as her mother tongue and Czech because it was the official language. In her village, the young girl showed her concern for children at an early age and in fact became a kindergarten teacher. "I love children. There was always a social worker in me ... Not a bad way to live your life," she said in a filmed interview three years before her death.[545] Her nieces and nephews confirm that even in her youth, she was independent, self-confident, of good character, disciplined, creative and warm-hearted. Her ideas were often ahead of her time. Her niece Ruth Lemco remembers, "She was young and refreshing, most of her life eager to learn and experience, often lecturing but with a tremendous sense of humor."[546] At barely twenty, she left her parental home for Switzerland where she became a riding instructor at a famous girls' boarding school. As a nanny in Paris and in Stanisławów, Galicia[547] between 1936 and 1938 she learned French and Polish and later added English and Hebrew. According to her niece, "Greta was very good at her job. Those kids loved her a great deal and came to visit her often in later years."[548]

In May 1939, Greta and three of her older siblings and their families immigrated to London; a brother and a sister went to Palestine. Thus, they managed to escape from the German troops soon to invade and occupy their Moravian homeland. Their parents remained behind in Czechoslovakia and were murdered in 1943 by the Nazis.[549]

In London, Greta Fischer first helped out in her brother's furrier business sewing leather hats and gloves for the British army. "I was lucky," Fischer later wrote of her war years in London. Then she worked as a nanny and a nursery school teacher in the Foundling Site and in the Hocrato Road Day Nursery,[550] institutions for children traumatized by war.[551] In neighboring Hampstead, Anna Freud, daughter of the founder of psychoanalysis, was pioneering development of trauma therapy for children. "Contact with Anna Freud ... made a deep impression on me and helped me to better understand [the children's behavior],"[552] she wrote. "Separation from their families, as well as the problems of families torn apart by war, was painful for everyone. In myself, it provoked a sincere desire to help."[553] Greta Fischer remained in touch with Anna Freud and adopted some of her approaches and ideas about treatment. At a time when the importance of early childhood bonding with the mother, parent or other steady caregiver had hardly been recognized, Anna Freud was already urging that therapy be linked to care in family-type groups. Her knowledge of psychology would strongly influence Greta Fischer's later work with child survivors of the Holocaust in Kloster Indersdorf.

Given "what [she] had heard about Germany," at the end of the war she volunteered for the UNRRA to help overcome the "devastation" and challenges facing reconstruction in Europe.[554] In the International D.P. Children's Center Kloster Indersdorf (Dachau county) she did her best with the UNRRA team to ensure that youngsters who had been uprooted, orphaned and traumatized during the Holocaust received urgent basic care. Convinced that human contact is essential for healing, she encouraged her coworkers to do their utmost in dealing with each of the infants and children as individuals with unique physical, psychological and spiritual needs. She listened attentively when the young survivors talked to her, whenever they repeated their devastating experiences, and requisitioned whatever could help smooth their paths back to life. "It was astonishing to see what a miracle could be worked for children orphaned by the Holocaust when the right thing was done," – Fischer's credo.

Greta Fischer with children in Kloster Indersdorf (1945).

Then in the summer of 1946, the Children's Center moved from Indersdorf to Prien on Chiemsee. She now found herself directing the International Children's Center Hotel Kronprinz Prien together with 40 mainly Central and Eastern European co-workers[555] and continued to promote rehabilitation of these traumatized children. On behalf of the UNRRA, she also worked in the Jewish orphanage in Ansbach and in Bad Reichenhall.

In October 1947, "for personal reasons," she ended her contract with the UNRRA[556] to continue to devote herself to "her children." In the summer of 1948, Greta Fischer accompanied 100 young Holocaust survivors to Canada to assist them in integrating into Canadian society. A characteristic anecdote concerning events on the vessel *Rudnik* survives: since there were no adequate medical personnel on board, Fischer helped at the birth of a baby and then saw to it that the youthful passengers under her care knitted clothing for the infant.

On arrival in Toronto, the young people went to live with Jewish families throughout Canada while Greta Fischer had to travel on to Montreal to take up her new position with the Jewish Family and Child Welfare Agency. This separation was shocking for both sides, and Fischer had first to prove her abilities as a social worker to the satisfaction of her new employer. Then, for the next three and a half years, she led a temporary shelter serving not only child survivors from Europe, but also homeless young Canadians. As the number of European refugees receded, she spent two more years in search of families willing to adopt or take foster children into their homes. "It was enriching to me, being able to assist these youngsters find themselves and start new lives but I also learned that the will to help isn't enough. You also need specific knowledge and formal training,"[557] — the reason she gave for enhancing her already proven experience as a social worker with a master's degree in social work.

During her enrollment in a two-year Master's in Education program at McGill University,[558] she also set up a counseling service at Montreal Children's Hospital for pre-school children with psychological problems. This pilot project developed into a psychotherapeutic day-care clinic for children with serious emotional challenges. After completing her MA in 1955, she directed the day-care clinic, trained staff, and had considerable success in treating autistic patients. Looking to broaden her experience, she worked from 1958 to 1960 for the JOINT in Casablanca, Morocco, where she was responsible for training social workers and teachers to work with groups of preschoolers and children. She also instructed mothers in child care and nutrition. "The country itself, the different cultures and customs and the need of the people made high demands on me. It challenged everything I ever learned in Social Work and at the same time it validated the most basic principles of Social Work."[559]

The JOINT transferred Greta Fischer for three years to Israel where she worked with the Ministry of Health to assess and help improve institutions for the handicapped, to train staff and cooperate in founding "Work Villages"[560] for people with cognitive disabilities. Meanwhile, she also volunteered to counsel initiatives and government aid projects concerned with caring for children with disabilities as well as with in-home care for seniors and the integration of immigrants from Iraq, Morocco and Egypt.

In 1963 Greta Fischer returned to Canada where for the next two years she directed the Social Work Department at St. Justine's Hospital in Montreal. Here she created a multidisciplinary team of social workers and therapists and developed special programs for victims of thalidomide and their families.

In July 1965 Greta Fischer moved permanently to Israel. There she was hired by Jerusalem's Hadassah Hospital, the largest and most prominent in the nation, where she built up the Social Work Department and directed it until her retirement in 1980. As a faculty member at the Paul Baerwald School of Social Work, she helped prepare students for their future profession. Fischer was a doer; she saw to it that patients who were released from the hospital continued to receive care once they were at home. She set up a telephone hotline for cancer patients. She also founded "Melabev," today the leading Israeli aid organization for dementia patients and their families; she initiated short-term care facilities and senior citizens' clubs. Everywhere she inspired people to offer empathetic support to others. The special place of social work in Israeli hospitals is her legacy.[561]

When Greta Fischer retired at age 70 in Jerusalem, she finally found the time to reconsider her experiences in postwar Germany, to look over her reports from Indersdorf, and to reflect on and summarize them.⁵⁶² With hindsight, she found the experience she had had with young, orphaned and displaced children in Kloster Indersdorf decisive for her life: "The pressure of work and the emotional strain [were] great and at that time I was not conscious of the impact this experience made on me. [Today], however, I know it was a lasting one and that I never witnessed greater suffering. ... It was the dignity and strength and the way people dealt with their difficult situation that impressed me most and which taught me unforgettable lessons."⁵⁶³ Her whole life she remained in awe of the "indomitable" will to live and resilience of those in her care despite all their unspeakable experiences.

Greta Fischer (3rd from left) receiving the Eshel Prize for social service to Israel, 1985.

Greta Fischer never married and had no children, but she accompanied the children of her many friends for years as they grew up, served as both a soul mate and someone they could look up to, and communicated her own playful joy in action with warmth, good humor, grace and more than a few good ideas.⁵⁶⁴ She also stayed in touch with some of "her children" from Kloster Indersdorf for the rest of her life, for instance with Kurt Klappholz[565] and Jakob (Jack) Hecht.[566] In 1985, she addressed the "Canadian Gathering of Jewish Holocaust Survivors and Their Children" in Ottawa and was honored for her significant contribution to their rehabilitation. "Greta's story can only show that she lived for the sake of others. She was a courageous woman who often fought against ignorance; but she was successful in her endeavors to help others to help themselves,"[567] as her niece Ruth Lemco summarizes her aunt's life.

In all the institutions that Greta Fischer founded in Israel, numerous volunteers remain active to this day. Even twenty years after her death, many Israelis remember with deep respect Greta Fischer's dedication to people of different religions and nationalities. In January 2010, to celebrate the 100th anniversary of her birth, a group of about 70 friends in Jerusalem organized a one-day conference in her honor. Speakers represented the many different institutions she had inspired or founded. Most of the approximately 160 participants had personal memories of Greta Fischer's exemplary work. For many, she was a passionate and fearless model ally to children and all in need of help. Her successor as head of the social work department at Hadassah Hospital[568] sees Greta Fischer as "always good at discovering whatever might work to heal." "She brought culture shock to Hadassah Hospital, Europe from its best side."[569] Her former co-workers always felt that she recognized their value, motivated them to give their best, and in difficult times offered unconditional support. The question, "What would Greta do in this situation?" remains for her friends, even decades after her death, a truly helpful approach to making difficult decisions.[570]

The Canadian author Fraidie Martz, who studied education in Montreal with Fischer, explained her success: "Greta was blessed with astonishing energy and she had an unshakable conviction that all children, no matter how wounded, have a capacity, possibly hidden or suppressed by hard times, to win back the strength to manage in life. But for this to work, the child must be loved."[571] This insight did not crumble under the horrible events of the past century but instead was strengthened. The passionate social worker Greta Fischer embodied and lived it.

When in 2011 the Special Education Center in Dachau was named the Greta Fischer School, it was to preserve the ideal model that Greta Fischer represented for the younger generation of teachers and students. "She applied a modern therapeutic method in her teaching and always focused on the whole child," the school's director, Gabriele Oswald-Kammerer said to explain the school's chosen name. "Children with special needs must have special attention or nothing will work."[572]

Resources and Works Cited

Archives

AJJDC, Givat Joint Archives, Jerusalem
Archive of the Dachau Concentration Camp Memorial
Archive of the Flossenbürg Concentration Camp Memorial
Author's archive (aa-archive)
Central Zionist Archives, Jerusalem (CZA)
Greta Fischer's personal legacy (GFL) (aa-archives)
Hashomer Hatzair Archives, Kibbutz Givat Haviva, Israel
Heimatvereins Indersdorf e. V., archive, Markt Indersdorf (Archive H.I.)
Imperial War Museum, London (IWM)
Institut für Zeitgeschichte, Munich (IfZ)
International Tracing Service Archives, Bad Arolsen (ITS)
Markt Indersdorf registry office, Markt Indersdorf
Museum of Jewish Heritage, New York (MJH)
Stadtarchiv Neunburg vorm Wald, Germany
United Nations Archives and Records Center, New York (UN Archives)
US Holocaust Memorial Museum, Washington D.C. (USHMM)
Vancouver Holocaust Education Center

Newspapers

Salek **Benedikt**, Wir fahren nach England, in: *Journal 26*, Holocaust Survivors '45 Aid Society, 2002.
J. **E.**, Die Kinder von Indersdorf, in: *Neue Zeitung*, October 25, 1945.
Ruth S. **Feder**, Young DP Victims of the German War leave UNRRA child center for Russia, in: UNRRA team news, Vol. 2 No.1, DP Operations Germany, January 8, 1947.
Daniela **Gorgs**, Im Geist der Liebe, in: *Süddeutsche Zeitung*, Dachau regional supplement, July 2, 2010.
Kurt **Klappholz**, Morris (Mojze) Besserman (obituary), in: *Journal 9*, Holocaust Survivors '45 Aid Society, 1981.

Walter P. **Kloeck**, Die Kinder von Indersdorf, in: *Süddeutsche Zeitung*, December 4, 1945.

Peter Lane **Taylor**, Off the Face of the Earth. The remarkable story of a group of Holocaust survivors who hid in one of the world's largest caves. http://www.aish.com/63053312.html

Films

Hanus **Burger**, Die Waisen von Dachau/The Orphans of Dachau, Post-War Newsreels, Imperial War Museum, London, Film and Video Archive, WPN 242-WIF 25.
Greta **Fischer's** filmed interview, private video, Canada 1985, aa-archive
Herb **Krosney**, The Boys. Triumph Over Adversity, DVD, Krosney Productions 2006.
Jack **Kuper**, Children of the Storm, VHS tape, Kuper Productions, Toronto 2001.
Yvonne **Menne**, Das Lager der verlassenen Kinder. Lindenfels, die Überlebenden und der Exodus. TV documentary, Hessischer Rundfunk 2000.
Jim G. **Tobias**, Die vergessenen Kinder von Strüth, TV documentary, Medienwerkstatt Franken, Nuremberg 2001.
Bettina **Witte**/Anna Andlauer, Aus der Hölle ins Leben, TV documentary, ZDF 2009.
Fred **Zinnemann**, The Search (German: Die Gezeichneten), USA/Switzerland 1948.

Books

Anna **Andlauer**, Die internationalen Kinderzentren Kloster Indersdorf 1945–1948, in: Norbert Göttler, ed. Nach der »Stunde Null«. Stadt und Landkreis Dachau 1945 bis 1949, Munich 2008.
Anna **Andlauer**, Greta Fischer und die Arbeit mit jungen Holocaust Überlebenden im »International D.P. Children's Center Kloster Indersdorf« 1945–46, in: Jim G. Tobias/Peter Zinke, eds, nurinst 2010. Beiträge zur deutschen und jüdischen Geschichte, Nuremberg 2010.

175 Jahre **Barmherzige Schwestern** in Bayern. 1832 bis 2007, Munich 2007.

Yehuda **Bauer**, Flight and Rescue. Brichah, New York 1970.

John **Belsher**, Surviving Auschwitz to Buchenwald - The Autobiography of Irving Klein, Charleston, SC, 2012.

Wolfgang **Benz**/Barbara Distel, eds, Flossenbürg. Das Konzentrationslager Flossenbürg und seine Außenlager, Munich 2007.

Walter **Beringer**, Die UNRRA im Kloster Indersdorf, in: Jahresbericht der Realschule Vinzenz von Paul, Indersdorf 1994/95.

Michael **Brenner**, Nach dem Holocaust. Juden in Deutschland 1945–1950, Munich 1995.

Christina **Dietrich**, »... ich wundere mich, dass ich überlebt habe«, in: Jim G. Tobias/Peter Zinke, eds. nurinst 2010. Beiträge zur deutschen und jüdischen Geschichte, Nuremberg 2010.

Robert **Domes**, Nebel im August. Die Lebensgeschichte des Ernst Lossa, Munich 2008.

Nathan **Durst**, Eine Herausforderung für Therapeuten. Psychotherapie mit Überlebenden der Shoa, in: Ludewig Kedmi/Miriam Victory Spiegel/Silvie Tyrangiel, eds. Revital. Das Trauma des Holocaust zwischen Psychologie und Geschichte, Zürich 2002.

Angelika **Eder**, Flüchtige Heimat. Jüdische Displaced Persons in Landsberg am Lech 1945 bis 1950, Munich 1998.

Albert **Ehrhardt**, Chronik des Marktes Stamsried, Stamsried 2006.

Jack **Eisner**, Die Happy Boys. Eine jüdische Band in Deutschland 1945 bis 1949, Berlin 2004.

Solly **Ganor**, Aufleben 1945, Munich 2010.

Jacqueline D. **Giere**, Wir sind unterwegs, aber nicht in der Wüste. Erziehung und Kultur in den Jüdischen Displaced Persons Lagern der Amerikanischen Zone im Nachkriegsdeutschland 1945–1949, Diss., Frankfurt a. M. 1993.

Martin **Gilbert**, The Boys. The Story of 732 Young Concentration Camp Survivors, New York 1996.

Katrin **Greiser**, Die Todesmärsche von Buchenwald. Räumung, Befreiung und Spuren der Erinnerung, Göttingen 2008.

Christoph **Hackelsberger**, Kloster Indersdorf. Realschule Vinzenz von Paul, Munich 2006.

Hans **Holzhaider**, Die Kinderbaracke von Indersdorf, in: Wolfgang Benz Barbara Distel, eds. Dachauer Hefte 3, Dachau 1987.
Wolfgang **Jacobmeyer**, Vom Zwangsarbeiter zum heimatlosen Ausländer, Göttingen 1985.
Roman **Kent**, Courage Was My Only Option, New York 2008.
Hans **Keilson**, Sequentielle Traumatisierung bei Kindern. Untersuchung zum Schicksal jüdischer Kriegswaisen, Gießen 1979.
Hans **Keilson**, Das »Nachher« der Überlebenden, in: Wolfgang Benz Barbara Distel, eds. Dachauer Hefte 8, Dachau 1992.
Angelika **Königseder**/Juliane Wetzel, Lebensmut im Wartesaal: Die jüdischen DPs (Displaced Persons) im Nachkriegsdeutschland, Frankfurt a. M. 1994.
Eugen **Kogon**, Der SS-Staat, Munich 1974.
Dietrich **Kohlmannslehner**, »... wohnen auf der verfluchten deutschen Erde«. Jüdisches Leben in Südhessen nach 1945, Darmstadt 1998.
Eva **Kolinsky**, After the Holocaust. Jewish Survivors in Germany After 1945, London 2004.
Angela **Kühner**, Trauma und kollektives Gedächtnis, Gießen 2008.
Patricia De **Landtsheer**, Bewaar Altijd Een Stukje Brood, Antwerpen 2001.
Georg **Lilienthal**, Der »Lebensborn e.V.«. Ein Instrument nationalsozialistischer Rassenpolitik, Frankfurt a. M. 1993.
Fraidie **Martz**, Open Your Hearts. The Story of the Jewish War Orphans in Canada, Montreal 1996.
Fraidie **Martz**, Fischer, Greta (1909–1988), in: Anne Commire/Deborah Klezmer/Barbara Morgan, eds. Women in World History, Vol. 5, Waterford 2000.
Sarah **Moskovitz**, Love Despite Hate. Child Survivors of the Holocaust and their Adult Lives, New York 1983.
Margarete **Myers Feinstein**, Holocaust Survivors in Postwar Germany, 1945–1957, New York 2010.
Jörg **Skriebeleit**, Erinnerungsort Flossenbürg. Akteure, Zäsuren, Geschichtsbilder, Göttingen 2009.
Zahava Szász **Stessel**, Snow Flowers. Hungarian Jewish Women in an Airplane Factory, Markkleeberg, Germany. Madison, NJ, 2009.

Peter Lane **Taylor**, Christos Nicola, The Secret of Priest's Grotto. A Holocaust Survival Story, Minneapolis, 2007.
Jim G. **Tobias**, Vorübergehende Heimat im Land der Täter. Jüdische DP-Camps in Franken 1945–1949, Nuremberg 2002.
Jim G. **Tobias**, Die jüdischen DP-Lager Pürten (Waldkraiburg) und das Kinderlager Aschau, in: Jim G. Tobias/Peter Zinke, eds. nurinst 2004. Beiträge zur deutschen und jüdischen Geschichte, Nuremberg 2004.
Jim G. **Tobias**/Nicola Schlichting, Heimat auf Zeit. Jüdische Kinder in Rosenheim 1946–47, Nuremberg 2006.
Juliane **Wetzel**, Jüdisches Leben in München 1945–1951. Durchgangsstation oder Wiederaufbau?, Munich 1987.
Juliane **Wetzel**, Ziel: Erez Israel. Jüdische DP-Kinder als Hoffnungsträger für die Zukunft, in: Jüdisches Museum Frankfurt, ed. Rettet die Kinder, Frankfurt a. M. 2003.
George **Woodbridge**, UNRRA. The History of the United Nations Relief and Rehabilitation Administration, New York 1950.

Illustrations

AJJDC, Givat Joint Archives, Jerusalem: Page 177.
Anna **Andlauer**, Weichs, Germany: Pages 5, 84 (r), 163 (l).
Salek **Benedikt**, UK, aa-archive: Pages 19, 32 (l).
Zoltán **Farkas**, USA, aa-archive: Pages 88 (l), 149.
Greta **Fischer**'s personal legacy, aa-archive: Pages 28 (r), 32 (r), 34 (r), 35 (l), 40 (l), 65 (l), 77 (l), 78, 130 (l), 132 (r), 141 (l), 172.
Ulrich **Fritz**, Flossenbürg Concentration Camp Memorial: Page 166.
The **Ghetto** Fighters' House, Archives, Israel: Pages 137, 155.
Norbert **Habschied**, Dachau, Germany: Page 12.
Martin **Hecht**, Israel, aa-archive: Page 131.
Heimatverein Indersdorf e. V., archive, Markt Indersdorf: Pages 9, 17, 21, 22, 47, 158.
Eric **Hitter**, Belgium, aa-archive: Page 164.
Steve **Israeler**, USA, aa-archive: Page 140.
Niels-Peter **Joergensen**, Dachau, Germany: Page 186.
Ester **Katz**, Israel, aa-archive: Page 154.
Irving **Klein**, USA, aa-archive: Pages 71, 95, 139.

Abram **Leder**, Israel, aa-archive: Pages 26, 169.
Dietrich **Mittler**, MiPictures: Page 170.
Museum of Jewish Heritage, Archives, New York: Pages 41 (r).
National Archives and Records Administration, Washington D.C.: Page 49.
Hans **Neumann**, UK, aa-archive: Page 160.
Chana **Porat**, Israel, aa-archive: Pages 114, 144.
Michael V. **Roth**, USA, aa-archive: Page 168.
Mendel **Tropper**, Israel, aa-archive: Page 92.
United Nations Archives and Records Center, New York: Pages 38, 44, 46, 50, 51, 56, 80, 125.
US Holocaust Memorial Museum, Washington D. C.: Pages 28 (l), 29 (l), 30, 31, 40 (r), 45, 53, 57 (r), 60, 61, 65 (r), 67, 68, 72, 74, 84 (l), 85, 86 (r), 88 (r), 102, 103, 106, 110, 111, 116, 117, 118, 128, 135, 141 (r), 146, 150, 163 (l), 165 (l), 174.
Vancouver Holocaust Education Center: Pages 1, 16, 24, 29 (r), 34 (l), 35 (r), 36, 41 (l), 42, 54, 55, 57 (l), 58, 62, 63, 75, 77 (r), 86 (l), 105, 112, 113, 119, 121, 123, 127, 130 (r), 132 (r), 145.
Andrew **Wakeford**, Saarbrücken, Germany: Page 165 (r).
Roman **Weinstock**, Israel, aa-archive: Page 83.
Uta **Zelk**, Canada, aa-archive: Page 96.

About the Author

Anna Andlauer, born in 1950, majored in English, sociology and art history. During her years as a high school teacher she began to guide tour groups to Dachau Concentration Camp Memorial, and this focus on contemporary history eventually found expression in exhibitions and newspaper articles on the history of the Dachau Camp. She is the author of *Du, ich bin der Häftling mit der Nr. 1* on Claus Bastian, the first registered prisoner at this camp. While teaching in German schools and participating in teaching exchanges in the UK and the USA, she always invited Holocaust survivors to address her classes. Since 2008 she has specialized on the International D.P. Children's Center Kloster Indersdorf, tracing survivors now spread all over the world who had been cared for at the center in the immediate post-war era. She has interviewed them and invited them back to visit "their cloister," meet each other and local people, and talk about their experiences.

Notes

[1] Fraidie Martz, "Fischer, Greta (1909-1988)" in Anne Commire, Deborah Klezmer, Barbara Morgan, eds. *Women in World History* . Vol. 5. Waterford, 2000. 545-549. There is a mistake in Greta Fischer's birth year. It was 1910.
[2] Hans Keilson, "Das ‚Nachher' der Überlebenden," in Wolfgang Benz, Barbara Distel, eds. *Dachauer Hefte 8*. Dachau 1992, p. 33.
[3] Greta Fischer Papers relating to Kloster Indersdorf displaced children's center and to UNRRA's postwar work in Europe, January 1946. US Holocaust Memorial Museum (USHMM), RG-19.034, 1946. (GFP, 1946).
[4] At last, in 1980-1982, she found the time to reflect on her team's work during the immediate post-war period. Her niece Lilo Plaschkes gave these writings to the US Holocaust Memorial Museum after Fischer's death. The gift included the original script, lists of names, and photos of the children. (Greta Fischer Papers relating to Kloster Indersdorf displaced children's center and to UNRRA's postwar work in Europe, USHMM, RG-19.034*06/2 of 2, 1982). (GFP, 1982). Greta Fischer's nephew and legacy curator Micha Plaschkes (Israel) and her Canadian friend Fraidie Martz gave the Author Greta Fischer's reports, personal letters, documents, and a number of photos from Kloster Indersdorf, Greta Fischer's legacy (GFL). They are now in the Author's archive, aa-archive.
[5] Greta Fischer, personal letters, GFL.
[6] Greta Fischer. From Awareness – to Action, Speech at the Canadian Gathering of Jewish Holocaust Survivors and Their Children, Ottawa, 1985, GFL.
[7] Greta Fischer, Letter to Esther Halevi, Tel Aviv 1986, GFL.
[8] Jim G. Tobias, Nicola Schlichting, *Heimat auf Zeit. Jüdische Kinder in Rosenheim 1946-47*, Nuremberg, Antogo, 2006, p. 10.
[9] Dietrich Kohlmannslehner, „... wohnen auf der verfluchten deutschen Erde," *Jüdisches Leben in Südhessen nach 1945*, Darmstadt 1998, especially the chapter on Lindenfels – a "Children's Colony."Yvonne Menne, *Das Lager der verlassenen Kinder Lindenfels, die Überlebenden und der Exodus*. TV documenta-

ry, Hessischer Rundfunk 2000.Jim G. Tobias. *Die vergessenen Kinder vom Strüth*, TV Documentary, Medienwerkstatt Franken, Nuremberg 2001.Julianne Wetzel, „Ziel: Erez Israel. Jüdische DP-Kinder als Hoffnungsträger für die Zukunft," in Jüdisches Museum Frankfurt, ed. *Rettet die Kinder*. Frankfurt/Main 2003, p. 75 ff.Jim G. Tobias, Die jüdischen DP Lager Pürten (Waldkraiburg) und das Kinderlager Aschau, in Jim G. Tobias/Peter Zinke, eds. *nurinst 2004. Beiträge zur deutschen und jüdischen Geschichte*. Nuremberg, 2004, p. 129 ff.

[10] Tobias/Schlichting, *Heimat auf Zeit*, p. 11.

[11] Anna Andlauer, Die internationalen Kinderzentren Kloster Indersdorf 1945-1948, in Norbert Göttler, ed. *Nach der »Stunde Null«. Stadt und Landkreis Dachau 1945 bis 1949*. Munich 2008.

[12] Anna Andlauer, Greta Fischer und die Arbeit mit jungen Holocaust-Überlebenden im „International D.P. Children's Center Kloster Indersdorf" 1945-46, in Jim G. Tobias/Peter Zinke, eds. *nurinst 2010. Beiträge zur deutschen und jüdischen Geschichte*, Nuremberg 2010.

[13] Bettina Witte/Anna Andlauer, *Aus der Hölle ins Leben*, TV documentary, ZDF 2009.

[14] Only the Soviets refused to set up D.P. camps. See Jim G. Tobias, *Vorübergehende Heimat im Land der Täter. Jüdische DP-Camps in Franken, 1945-1949*. Nuremberg 2002, p. 15.

[15] The Allies calculated that in Western and Northern Europe, they would be dealing with more than 11 million DPs and refugees. "Of this number, 8,935,400 were outside their home countries, while 2,397,300 were displaced within their nations' boundaries," although German refugees were not included in these figures. The victors took into consideration that the largest number of DPs (7,725,000) would be found in the area of the German Reich. Wolfgang Jacobmeyer, *Vom Zwangsarbeiter zum Heimatlosen Ausländer*, Göttingen 1985, p. 24.

[16] For more on the history of the UNRRA, see George Woodbridge, *UNRRA. The History of the United Nations Relief and Rehabilitation Administration*, 3 Volumes, New York 1950.

[17] Greta Fischer was a Jew from Moravia/Czechoslovakia. Her mother tongue was German; she also spoke Czech, French, English and some Polish. A certified kindergarten teacher, during the

war she worked in London in Anna Freud's circle developing trauma therapy for children. For more about her life, see the appendix, Greta Fischer – Stages in a Life.

[18] Greta Fischer's filmed interview. Private video, Canada, 1985, the Author's archive (aa-archive). (GF film)

[19] The UNRRA workers called all young people up to the age of 25 "children."

[20] Qtd. in Tobias/Schlichting, *Heimat auf Zeit*, p. 8.

[21] GF film.

[22] GFP, 1946, p. 1.

[23] GFP, 1982, p. 12.

[24] Admission of Children, p. 2 f. In Displaced Persons – Children – Repatriation and Resettlement 8/10/1945 – 17/12/1945, UN Archives S-0437-0017-06.

[25] Dr. Baumberg, Assistant to the Chief Welfare Officers in Bavaria, Reislinger Straße 10 in Munich reported these children to the Team 182. Their mothers (and some fathers) had been foreign forced laborers who were still working in Germany or had already been repatriated. The identities of many children were unclear. If they happened to be Austrian, Hungarian or Romanian, it was also uncertain whether they fell under the UNRRA mandate and could be helped since these nations were "ex-enemies." Admission of Children, p. 1, UN Archives.

[26] Ibid.

[27] GFP, 1946, p. 1 f.

[28] Bayerischer Landesverband für Wander- und Heimatdienst, registered Nazi government agency, Munich, responsible for all German homeless, needy people in Bavaria.

[29] In 1938 the nunnery Kloster Indersdorf "was shut down by the head of the district branch of the Nazi party. Education in Catholic institutions was not well-viewed in the Third Reich. During the war the building was used by the NSV (Nationalsozialistische Volkswohlfahrt, a Nazi welfare agency) as a home for the *Kinderlandverschickung*, an agency charged with removing German children from the bombed out cities and placing them in rural homes." Christoph Hackelsberger, *Kloster Indersdorf, Realschule Vinzenz von Paul*, Munich 2006, p. 10.

[30] Admission of Children, p. 1, UN Archives.

[31] The UNRRA Team 182 used this term; it is retained by many English-speaking ex-residents today.
[32] GFP, 1946, p. 4.
[33] Admission of Children, p. 1, UN Archives.
[34] GFP, 1982, p. 5. Later on, all the larger DP camps in Bavaria like Föhrenwald and Feldafing had separate children's houses; in July 1945, however, in Kloster Indersdorf the first mixed center for children and youth in the US Zone of Germany opened its doors. In the fall of 1945 the DP camp Föhrenwald would become the central camp for all Jewish children in Bavaria. Miriam Warburg, *Conditions of Jewish Children in a Bavarian Rehabilitation Camp*, October 1945, Institut für Zeitgeschichte, Munich (IfZ) Fi 01.81. Later camps exclusively for Jewish children were created in Aschau, Bayrisch Gmain, Indersdorf, Lindenfels, Prien, Pürten (Mühldorf), Rosenheim, Strüth (Ansbach), Traunstein, Ulm and Wartenberg. Angelika Königseder, Juliane Wetzel, *Lebensmut im Wartesaal. Die jüdischen DPs (Displaced Persons) im Nachkriegsdeutschland*, Frankfurt a. M., 1994, p. 247 ff.
[35] "The typical administrative unit for an average camp with 3000 inhabitants was the so-called team: eight members in comparable officers' ranks (director, assistant director, and clerks responsible for supplies, food, storage, welfare, and health), 6 members charged with specific duties who, in camps run by the military, were chosen from enlisted ranks (personnel for secretariat and administration, assistants to the head of the welfare department, nurses, cooks, and two drivers)." Jacobmeyer, *Vom Zwangsarbeiter zum heimatlosen Ausländer*, p. 33.
[36] GF film.
[37] Jean Margaret Henshaw had been relieved of her duties as chief administrator of the large DP camp Föhrenwald due to her anti-Zionism that led to "considerable misunderstandings with the largely Zionist-oriented Jewish inmates." Königseder/Wetzel, *Lebensmut im Wartesaal*, pp. 102 & 256.
[38] After his death, André Marx's papers were given to the Museum of Jewish Heritage (MJH) in New York City. They include numerous letters and photos of children and youths in Kloster Indersdorf 1945-46.

[39] Kurt Klappholz, Gereimte Prosa, Danklied für das UNRRA-Team 182. Kloster Indersdorf, October 13, 1945, GFL.
[40] Team 182 – Kloster Indersdorf – 3rd Army, UN Archives, S-0425-0059-07.
[41] Recommendations, p. 4. Displaced Persons – Children – Repatriation and Resettlement 8/10/1945 – 17/12/1945, UN Archives, S-0437-0017-06.
[42] Admission of Children, p. 1, UN Archives.
[43] UNRRA Team Report, Team No. 182, Director Lillian D. Robbins, Kloster Indersdorf near Dachau, September 15, 1945, p. 1, UN Archives, S-0436-0039-01.
[44] Minutes from July 11, 1945, *Die Übernahme des Jugendheims in Kloster Indersdorf*, Legacy of Centa Probstmayr, Heimatverein Indersdorf e.V., archive.
[45] Letter from Sister Dolorosa to her Mother Superior, July 14, 1945, Archive H.I.
[46] Ibid.
[47] GF film.
[48] For the entire month of August 1945, these people appear on the UNRRA team's list of waged workers. D.P. Children's Center Kloster Indersdorf, Dachau County, UN Archives. Udi Witelson kindly made these documents available to the Author.
[49] Letter from Sister Dolorosa to her Mother Superior, 3 August 1945., Archive H.I.
[50] Recommendations, p. 2, UN Archives.
[51] GFP, 1982, p. 35.
[52] GFP, 1982, p. 11.
[53] GF film.
[54] GFP, 1946, p. 5.
[55] UNRRA Team Report, Team No. 182, September 15, 1945, UN Archives. Some of the DPs (14 DPs on March 30, 1946) also received payment from Indersdorf's mayor. UNRRA Monthly Team Report, March 30, 1946. UN Archives, S-0436-0039-02.
[56] Die UNRRA in der Marienanstalt in Kloster Indersdorf und der Weggangder Schwestern im August 1946, August 14, 1946, p. 6, Archive H.I.
[57] Recommendations, p. 1. UN Archives.

[58] In May, 1946, when a military "screening team" checked all residents, six grown-up DPs were disqualified. UNRRA Monthly Team Report, May 31, 1946, UN Archives, S-0436-0039-01. In July 1946 three more DPs were dismissed. "During this period the D.P. warehouseman Mr. A. M. was found by the investigation of German policemen to be involved in the black market in cooperation with two friends. They were all arrested and Mr. M. was sentenced to one year's imprisonment." UNRRA Monthly Team Report, July 15, 1946, UN Archives, S-0436-0039-01.
[59] Ibid.
[60] Dr. Martha Branscombe (1906-1997), for instance, in March 1946 in Indersdorf, was assigned to prepare the emigration of orphans to the USA. UNRRA Monthly Team Report, March 30, 1946, UN Archives. Following her tour of duty in Kloster Indersdorf she was made responsible for the "US Committee for the Care of European Children" headquartered in Frankfurt. Letter from Martha Branscombe to J.H. Whiting, August 15, 1946, UN Archives, S-0425-0464-12. From 1954-1965 she was the Chief of the United Nations Social Services Division in the UN Secretariat.
[61] Letter from J.H. Whiting, Zone Director to Dr. Raphael Lemkin, Advisor on Foreign Affairs, War Department, U.S.A. Location of United Nations' Children in the US Zone, June 12, 1946, p. 2-3 in Child Welfare, March 1, 1946 to July 31, 1946, UN Archives, S-0425-0064-03.
[62] Admission of Children, p. 1. UN Archives.
[63] Letter from Sister Dolorosa to her Mother Superior, August 3, 1945. Archive H.I.
[64] Ibid.
[65] United Nations Relief and Rehabilitation Administration, Subcommittee on Welfare for Europe, Psychological Problems of Displaced Persons, London, August 11, 1945, IfZ, FI 01.81.
[66] *Die UNRRA in der Marienanstalt*, p. 1, Archive H.I.
[67] Ibid.
[68] For young Jewish survivors, psychologists often use the concept "child survivors." See Nathan Durst, „Eine Herausforderung für Therapeuten. Psychotherapie mit Überlebenden der Shoa," *Revital. Das Trauma des Holocaust zwischen Psychologie und Ge-*

schichte. Eds. Ludewig Kedmi, Miriam Victory Spiegel, Silvie Tyrangiel. Zürich 2002, p. 95.

[69] Greta Fischer reports that the few non-Jewish survivors of concentration camps were mainly Polish youth who had been interned during the Warsaw Uprising in September 1944. GFP, 1946, n.p. She also calls the young Ukrainian Michael (Mike) Kolesnik a survivor of a concentration camp.

[70] Author's discussions with survivors at the survivors' reunion in Indersdorf, July 2008, July 2009, and April 2010. Notes, aa-archive.

[71] GFP, 1946, p. 12 f.

[72] GFP, 1946, p. 18. In discussions the Author had with Abram Warszaw (Alec Ward) in January 2008 and March 2009 in London, Greta Fischer's description was confirmed. Notes, aa-archive.

[73] GFP, 1982. p. 18.

[74] A satellite camp to Groß-Rosen where forced labor for Krupp took place.

[75] Author's interview with Halina Bryks (Chana Porat) in Afula (Israel) on January 16, 2010. Notes, aa-archive.

[76] Discussion between the Author and Miklos Roth (Michael V. Roth) at the Survivors' Reunion in Indersdorf, July 2008 and July 2009. Notes, aa-archive.

[77] At that time he was called Israel. He was the only survivor of his family. Notes, aa-archive.

[78] Alfred Buchführer's report from April 1945, Dok. 4, Stadtarchiv Neunburg vorm Wald. Today he lives in Florida.

[79] "A constant preoccupation with food," 1994, Newspaper article, David Klappholz's private archive. A copy was kindly given to the Author, aa-archive.

[80] Salek Benedikt, „Wir fahren nach England," in Journal 26, *Holocaust Survivors '45 Aid Society*. 2002. p. 6.

[81] Interview with Kurt Klappholz, Imperial War Museum, London (IWM), Session 9425, reel 25.

[82] P. H. Powers, an American officer, prepared this important document for Hans Neumann and the Hahn brothers. P. H. Powers, Assembly Center No. 93254, Deggendorf. Document from Hans Neumann's private collection. A copy was kindly giv-

en to the Author, aa-archive. The three youths arrived together in Indersdorf although Hans Neumann emigrated from there to the UK while the Hahn brothers went to America. Herbert Hahn died in a work accident when he was 28 years old. Walter Hahn and Hans Neumann saw each other again for the first time after 63 years at the Survivors' Reunion in Indersdorf, July 2008. Notes, aa-archive .

[83] GFP, 1982, p. 20.

[84] UNRRA Monthly Team Report, September 15, 1945, p. 3. UN Archives.

[85] Benedikt, "Wir fahren nach England," in Journal 26, *Holocaust Survivors '45 Aid Society*, 2002. p. 6.

[86] Copy of Zdzislaw Szymanek's letter of March 18, 1980, T/D-1060387, International Tracing Service, Bad Arolsen.

[87] GFP, 1946, I. (5) Children deported for Slave Labor, n. p.

[88] Lillian D. Robbins, "Refugees – who cares?" Speech to the annual conference of the "National Federation of Settlements" September 12, 1947, GFP, USHMM, RG-19.034*04.

[89] George Sedgin, Civ. Interpreter UNRRA Team 182, The Story of Alexander Orloff, Miscellaneous reports relating to displaced children, GFP, USHMM, RG-19.034*10.

[90] Report from William R. Edgerton, UNRRA Team 143, Passau, Miscellaneous reports relating to displaced children, ibid.

[91] GFP, 1946, p. 13 and I (4) Children in the Germanization Program, (n.p.)

[92] The organization N.S.V. (Nationalsozialistische Volksfürsorge) or Nazi 'Welfare'; the National Socialist Charity "Mother and Child"; the Lebensborn registered charity or the Office of Race and Settlement (Rasse- und Siedlungsamt) were involved in kidnapping and importing these youths. J. H. Whiting, Zone Director to Dr. Raphael Lemkin, Advisor on Foreign Affairs, War Department, U.S.A. Location of United Nations' children in the US Zone, June 12, 1946, p. 3, in Child Welfare, 1 March 1946 – 31 July 1946, UN Archives, S-0425-0064-03.

[93] Some of them were unequivocally German, others Polish. J. H. Whiting, Investigations regarding Importation and Germanization of United Nations' Children, April 12, 1946, p. 1. Ibid.

[94] "Bund Deutscher Mädel," National Socialist girls' organization which all 'Aryan' girls from 10 to 18 had to join.
[95] Telephone interview between the Author and Ursula Bowitz (née Weißmann), November 21, 2011, aa-archive.
[96] In 1921 as a result of the Treaty of Versailles, the eastern part of Upper Silesia, from where these girls came, had become Polish. When in 1939 Germany brought this area "home to the Reich," the German part of the population welcomed the occupation with joy. After the war ended in 1945 the entire Upper Silesian population became Polish.
[97] Robbins, "Refugees – who cares…"
[98] Report of 2nd Lieutenant F. Longchamps, Miscellaneous reports relating to displaced children, GFP, USHMM, RG 19.034*10.
[99] Ibid.
[100] Children of Unknown Nationality but Probably Eastern European, DP Children's Center Kloster Indersdorf, Welfare – Child – Correspondence, 30/3, 1946 – 15/8/1946, UN Archives, S-0425-0064-05.
[101] Claude Huet, born 14 July 1934, came with his brother Jean Huet, born 9 July 1932, to Indersdorf, List of Children with information on birthdates, parentage and probable nationality, GFP, USHMM, BG-19.034*II.
[102] GFP, 1946, 15. f.
[103] GF film.
[104] Hans Holzhaider, Die Kinderbaracke von Indersdorf, in Wolfgang Benz Barbara Distel, eds. *Dachauer Hefte 3*, Dachau 1987, p. 116 ff.
[105] Five children who survived the Indersdorf "Kinderbaracke" became residents in the Children's Center: Lene Walekirow (see photo on the cover) born on 25 June 1935 in Leningrad was registered in the "Kinderbaracke" on 22 November 1944. Georg Novodvorskoya, born on 19 December 1943 in Dachau, appeared at first half-starved, too small for his age, and generally in a pitiable state. He recovered quickly, however, and appeared to Greta Fischer as "a very happy child with a good constitution." Stanislaus Felus, born 23 March 1943, was placed on March 19, 1945 in the Indersdorf "Kinderbaracke" after having been in the transi-

tional camp in Dachau. His parents are unknown though likely Soviet citizens. At first he appeared to be highly disturbed, wanted never to be alone and feared the dark. Greta Fischer wrote: "A highly sensitive child, he must be handled with great care." Barbara Miroschnitschenko's birth year could only be estimated as 1943. She arrived on the same day as Stanislaus Felus, also from the transit camp in Dachau and probably also had Soviet parentage. At first, she, too, was half-starved, cried a great deal, and struck out with considerable aggression. In October 1945 she appeared to be somewhat more tranquil and satisfied. Jura Piatek, born on April 17, 1944, in Dachau had been in the "Kinderbaracke" since October 1, 1944. Of his mother Anastasia Piatek it is only known that she was born on April 14, 1909, in Poland; his father, Vladislaw Budzisz was also from Poland. Personsonenstandsbuch der Kinderbaracke Kloster Indersdorf, Standesamt Markt Indesdorf, Copy from Hans Holzhaider, aa-archive. Babies in Swiss List, Kloster Indersdorf, Notes by Miss Greta Fischerova, Welfare Office, October 31, 1945, GFL.

[106] Dachau was not only a concentration camp but also one of the estimated 50 Dulags in the Reich. A Dulag – short form of "Durchgangslager" or transit camp – was the first stop for foreigners being kidnapped for forced labor in Germany.

[107] Babies in Swiss List, GFL.

[108] GFP, 1946, p. 12.

[109] GFP, 1946, II. (5) Family relationships – Voluntary Separation (n.p.).

[110] Ruth S. Feder, Young DP Victims of the German War leave UNRRA child center for Russia, in UNRRA team news, DP operations Germany, January 8, 1947, GFL.

[111] The infants arrived on August 29, 1945, in Indersdorf and were supposed to be given back to their parents, most of whom were waiting for them in Poland. Eight of them would have to wait until the summer of 1946 to be repatriated from Prien to the Ukraine. Repatriation of Soviet Children at Kloster Indersdorf, U.N.R.R.A. Liaison Office Third US Army Headquarters, Heidelberg: APO 403, to Miss C. Heise, Zone Child Welfare Specialist, June 13, 1946, UN Archives, S-0425-0064-05.

[112] Lebensborn e.V. was a state-sponsored organization funded by the SS that wedded national socialist "race hygiene" to health ideology and promoted increasing the birth rate of "Aryan" children by encouraging out-of-wedlock sexual relations. "Lebensborn" was also in part responsible for kidnapping children from occupied territories. If they conformed to the SS racist "Aryan" criteria, their identities were hidden and they were put up for adoption by German families. At the end of the war, documents that identified the children were often destroyed. See Georg Lilienthal, Der "Lebensborn e.V." Ein Instrument nationalsozialistischer Rassenpolitik, Frankfurt a. M. 2003.

[113] GFP, 1946, p. 12.

[114] "Kriegskinder, Reisewege der Meuser Waisenkinder," Lydiane Gueit-Montchal, Directeure des Archives départementales de la Meuse, France, November 26, 2004, translated by Eleonore Philipp, Markt Indersdorf, Archive H.I.

[115] Walter P. Kloeck, Die Kinder von Indersdorf, in *Süddeutsche Zeitung*, December 4, 1945.

[116] GFP 1946, II. (a) Physical and Mental Manifestation of Prolonged Starvation, n. p.

[117] "In psychology, trauma is an extreme experience that happens unexpectedly and has corresponding after-effects, immediate and long term." Kristina Dietrich "... Ich wundere mich, dass ich überlebt habe" ("... I'm amazed that I survived.") In Jim G. Tobias/Peter Zinke, eds. *nurinst 2010. Beiträge zur deutschen und jüdischen Geschichte*, Nuremberg 2010, p. 27.

[118] GFP, 1982, p. 41.

[119] Dichlordiphenyltrichloroethane (DDT) is a durable and highly effective insect extermination product whose application at this time was not unusual. Its danger to humans would be discovered only later.

[120] GF film.

[121] At first there weren't enough teachers for Hungarian, Hebrew, English or vocational training. A library was started and games, crafts and singing were offered. A "tactical unit" of the Army showed a film. UNRRA Monthly Team Report, September 15, 1945, p. 9. UN Archives.

[122] Letter from Sister Dolorosa to her Mother Superior, September 20, 1945. Archive H. I.
[123] GFP, 1982, p. 40.
[124] GFP, 1982, p. 40.
[125] UNRRA Monthly Team Report, September 15, 1945, p. 9. UN Archives.
[126] GFP, 1982, p. 25.
[127] Genia Edlermann is today Jean Sugar and lives with her family in Canada. Telephone Interview with the Author, June 2008. Notes, aa-archive.
[128] GFP, 1982, p. 25.
[129] GF film.
[130] For instance, teachers and representatives of Jewish organizations in October 1946 in the DP camp Belsen discussed at their weekly meeting how the displaced children in their care could be raised to be independent, responsible, clean and mannerly while dining. Königseder and Wetzel, *Lebensmut im Wartesaal*, p. 190.
[131] GF film and GFP, 1982, p.26.
[132] GFP, 1946, p. 19-20.
[133] UNRRA Subcommittee on Welfare for Europe, Psychological Problems of Displaced Persons, p. 12, IfZ, F1.01.81.
[134] GFP, 1946, II. (8) Physical and Mental Manifestation of Prolonged Starvation, n.p.
[135] GFP, 1982, p. 39.
[136] GFP, 1946, II. (8) Physical and Mental Manifestation of Prolonged Starvation, n.p.
[137] Ibid.
[138] Ibid.
[139] GFP, 1982, p. 39.
[140] Afterward, Dr. Josef Unger practiced in Dachau for the rest of his life. He was known to sooth his patients by singing arias. Information from Ludwika Zaidenstadt on July 7, 2008 in Markt Indersdorf. Notes, aa-archive.
[141] UNRRA Monthly Team Report, September 15, 1945, p. 10. UN Archives.
[142] Interview with Kurt Klappholz, IWM, Reel 23.
[143] Robert Hamser, born on March 8, 1946, died on May 10, 1946; Raimunda Thomas, born on January 9, 1945, died on April

29, 1946. Death Certificates in the Markt Indersdorf registry office. The two-year-olds Walter Beausert and Hanna Curija, as well as the three-year-old Monica Charlier, were among the children who survived this serious disease.

[144] This 14-day quarantine was ordered on May 3, 1946, by Captain Fred Knoke, 2nd Battalion, 60th Infantry, Dachau. Letter from Jean Margaret Henshaw to Cornelia Heise, Zone Child Welfare Officer, May 13, 1946, p. 2. Archive of the Dachau Concentration Camp Memorial.

[145] Jean Margaret Henshaw in UNRRA Monthly Team Report, May 31, 1946.

[146] UNRRA Monthly Team Report, April 30, 1946, p. 4, UN Archives, S-0436-0039-01.

[147] J. E., Die Kinder von Indersdorf, in *Neue Zeitung*, October 25, 1945.

[148] Josef and Alfred Lamzek were born on July 21, 1945 in different places (probably during transport) in Lower Bavaria. Their parents were Olga Lamzek and Josef Kaluschna (more is unknown). Josef Lamzek died on October 28, 1945, of atrophy, Alfred Lamzek on November 8, 1945, of heart failure. Death Certificates in the Markt Indersdorf registry office.

[149] Die UNRRA in der Mariananstalt, p. 8, Archive H.I. The report mentions the deceased Lamzek brothers, two dead due to diphtheria (Robert Hamser, Raimunda Thomas), one infant that died of pneumonia and another as a result of inability to eat. Among the latter was Daniele Canale, born in Munich on February 13, 1945 to a Catholic mother, Madeline Canale of Belgium, and Georges Debievre. She died in Schwabing Hospital in Munich on March 3, 1946.

[150] Roman Kniker (Kent), for instance, got hold of a fashionable leather coat, boots and even two gold watches for himself and his brother Leon. Roman Kent, *Courage Was My Only Option*, NY 2008, p. 134.

[151] GFP, 1982, p. 26 f.

[152] J. E., Die Kinder von Indersdorf, in *Neue Zeitung*, October 25, 1945.

[153] GF film.

[154] GF film.

[155] Warburg, Condition of Jewish Children, p. 7, IfZ, Fi 01.81.
[156] UNRRA Monthly Team Report, September 15, 1945, p. 8, UN Archives.
[157] GFP, 1982, p. 32. See also Lazar Kleinman's Remember me? profile, US Holocaust Memorial Museum, http://rememberme.ushmm.org.
[158] GFP,1982, p. 31.
[159] The UNRRA regulations allotted 30 square feet per person [about 2.8 square meters] if they had bunk beds and 36 square feet [about 3.4 square meters] in individual beds. UNRRA Monthly Team Report, September 15, 1945, p. 4. UN Archives.
[160] Ibid.
[161] Jean Margaret Henshaw to Cornelia Heise, Zone Child Welfare Officer, May 13, 1946, aa-archive.
[162] GFP, 1946, III (3), p. 2.
[163] GFP III (2).Content of Cultural & Recreational Expression, n.p.
[164] UNRRA Monthly Team Report, September 15, 1945, p. 2. UN Archives.
[165] XX Corps, Regional Office, UNRRA, APO 757, October 17, 1945, R.G. Mastrude, Acting Regional Supervisor, H. Zilka, Field Supervisor, Field Supervision Report, DP Children's Center, Kloster Indersdorf, Team 182, October 16, 1945, p. 3. UN Archives, S-0436-0016-02.
[166] Organisation and Morale Building in the Assembly Centres, UNRRA Review of the Month, 1945, October - November. UN Archives.
[167] GFP, 1982, p. 34.
[168] Jean Pierre Pellut (born December 15, 1943). List of Children with information on birthdates, parentage, and probable nationality, GFP. USHMM.
[169] GFP, 1946, p. 27.
[170] GFP, 1982, p. 24.
[171] GFP, 1982, p. 24-25.
[172] Recommendations, I. UN Archives.
[173] GFP 1946, single sheet, p. 2.
[174] UNRRA Monthly Team Report, July 15, 1946, Greta Fischerova, UN Archives, GFP, 1946, single sheet, p. 2.

[175] In December 1945 there were already five children's centers in the US Zone: Aglasterhausen (capacity 150-200), Kloster Indersdorf (capacity 200), Föhrenwald (capacity 900 Jewish girls and boys), Deggendorf (capacity 125-175), Wartenberg (capacity 150). UNRRA Headquarters U.S. Zone, Wiesbaden, Letter from Pearl Zimmerman (Chief Welfare Officer) to Relief Services Division, Central H.Q. for Germany, December 19, 1945, UN Archives, S-0437-0017-14.
[176] Die UNRRA in der Marienanstalt, p. 2, Archive H.I.
[177] UNRRA Subcommittee on Welfare for Europe, Psychological Problems of Displaced Persons, p.3, IfZ, F1 01.81.
[178] GFP, 1946, III (2) Content of Cultural and Recreational Expressions, n.p.
[179] Margarete Myers Feinstein. Holocaust Survivors in Postwar Germany, 1945-1957. NY, Cambridge University Press, 2010. p. 185. In Hanus Burger's cinema News Reel Show "The Orphans of Dachau" that reported on Kloster Indersdorf in December 1945, the commentator stated that first of all, the children should forget their frightful experiences. IWM, WPN 242-WIF 25.
[180] Margarete Myers Feinstein. *Holocaust Survivors in Postwar Germany*, p. 185.
[181] GF film.
[182] GF film.
[183] GF film.
[184] GF film
[185] GF film.
[186] Author's interview with Erwin Farkas at the Indersdorf Reunion in July 2008, aa-archive.
[187] Ibid.
[188] GFP, 1946, p. 18-19.
[189] GF film.
[190] GF film.
[191] Imre (Eric) Hitter. Email to the author. October 27, 2010, aa-archive.
[192] GFP, 1946, p. 16.
[193] American Jewish Joint Distribution Committee (JOINT for short) was an aid organization founded in 1914 in the USA to support Jews primarily in Europe.

[194] Warburg, Conditions of Jewish Children, p. 7, IfZ, Fi 01.81.
[195] Greta Fischer wrote in her 1946 report: "Attitude toward UNRRA and other center staff varied among all children according to the capabilities and sensibilities of the individual worker." III. (8) Attitude Toward Authority, single sheet, GFP, 1946.
[196] Recommendations, p. 3, UN Archives.
[197] Ibid.
[198] Petition to U.N.R.R.A. Headquarters [single sheet]. Signed by Roman and Leon Kniker (Kent), Erwin Farkas, Bernat Zelikovits (Zelk), Iwan Kisz (Irving Klein), Szlama Weichselblatt (Sol D. Wexler) and others against Helen Steiger's transfer. The letter was kindly given to the Author by Irving Klein and Udi Witelson (both in the USA), aa-archive.
[199] Wolfgang Jacobmeyer made this general assessment of DPs emotional state including adults. Jacobmeyer, *Vom Zwangsarbeiter zum heimatlosen Ausländer*, p. 50.
[200] Life at K.I., GF notes, GFL.
[201] GFP, 1982, p. 38.
[202] GFP, 1946, p. 29-30.
[203] GF film.
[204] GFP, 1946, p. 30.
[205] GFP, 1982, p. 38.
[206] Conversation with Bernat (Dov) Nasch in the baroque hall at Kloster Indersdorf, April 2010. Notes, aa-archive.
[207] GFP, 1982, p. 38.
[208] GFP, 1946, p. 10.
[209] GFP, 1982, p. 2.
[210] The Nazi agency Lebensborn "imported" foreign babies and toddlers and placed them in a series of private homes so that eventually their identities were lost when the German families adopted them. J. Whiting, Zone Director to War Crime Branch, Judge Advocate General, APO 633, US Army, Investigations regarding Importation and Germanization of United Nations' Children, April 12, 1946, UN Archives, S-0425-0064-03.
[211] GFP, 1982, p. 4.
[212] GFP, 1982, p. 13.
[213] GFP, 1946, p. 8.

[214] Zofia Karpuk is today Zofia Oglaza and lives in Lodz; she visited Kloster Indersdorf with her brother Janusz Karpuk in May 2009 and in May 2011. Notes, aa-archive.
[215] Ibid.
[216] Tabea Klara Langyte couldn't find out Sinaida Grussmann's date of birth or religious belief. The DP teacher discovered that Sinaida Grussmann had only spoken Latvian with her parents and grandparents and she assumed that the girl was Latvian because she was more fluent in this language than any other she was familiar with (Russian, German). When she was about five, the family moved to Russia. "The father was in the army. She has never seen him since. The family lived upstairs in a house with many other people. It was probably in the country since she remembers they had a cow. ... She had an older sister who died. She had no other brothers or sisters... She cannot recall a birthday celebration or a detail which could place the month of birth." Marion E. Hutton, Welfare Officer, to Miss Melba Foltz, UNRRA Tracing Bureau, Eastern Military District Headquarters, October 25, 1945. Sinaida Grussmann, Korrespondenz aus T/D Akte 1432050, ITS Archives Bad Arolsen.
[217] Years after the war ended, Martin Hecht, for instance, found his birth certificate in his Romanian hometown. In the meantime, however, another birthdate, which he kept, had been recorded in his documents. Conversation with the Author, Dachau, November 2008. Notes, aa-archive. After Abram Warszaw arrived in England in 1945, the Red Cross assisted him in finding his Buchenwald prisoner's records. They had written his birthday as March 1, 1927. Discussion between the Author and Alec Ward, London, March 2009, aa-archive. Miriam Warburg, in the DP Camp Föhrenwald in September 1945, noted that even many grown-ups had forgotten their birthdates. Warburg, Conditions of Jewish Children, p. 5, IfZ, Fi 01.81.
[218] GFP, 1982, p. 12 ff.
[219] Sedgin, The Story of Alexander Orloff, GFP, USHMM.
[220] Ibid.
[221] XX Corps Regional Office, UNRRA, APO 757, October 17, 1945. R.G. Mastrude, Acting Regional Supervisor, H. Zilka, Field Supervisor, Field Supervision Report, DP Children's Cen-

ter, Kloster Indersdorf, Team 182, October 16, 1945, p. 4. UN Archives, S-0437-0017-13.
[222] GFP, 1982, p. 17.
[223] In addition to Polish and Yugoslavian children, Greta Fischer names a group of 46 pupils from Czechoslovakia who in January 1945 had been violently separated from their parents and deported to work in Germany. GFP, 1982, p. 24.
[224] Report by Florian Kozlowski, Child Welfare Office Polish Red Cross, UN Archives, S-0437-0017-01.
[225] GFP, 1946, III. (1) Social-Moral Behavior, n.p.
[226] Jacobmeyer. *Vom Zwangsarbeiter zum heimatlosen Ausländer*, p. 110.
[227] GFP, 1982, p. 13 f.
[228] GFP, 1982, p. 13 f.
[229] GFP, 1982, p. 14.
[230] GF film.
[231] Repatriation of Soviet Children at Kloster Indersdorf, Pearl Morris, Liaison Officer to District Director, UNRRA, District No. 5, June 16, 1946, UN Archives, S-0425-0064-05.
[232] GFP, 1982, p. 23.
[233] UNRRA Monthly Team Report, July 15, 1946, Greta Fischerova, Welfare Supplementary Sheet, UN Archives.
[234] GFP, 1982, p. 32.
[235] Marion E. Hutton in Life at K. I., GF notes, GFL.
[236] The British government agreed to accept 1000 Jewish children under age 16 but in the end, only 732 young people immigrated to the UK, many of them older than 16. Martin Gilbert. *The Boys, the Story of 732 Young Concentration Camp Survivors*. NY, 1996.
[237] GF film.
[238] GF film.
[239] GFP, 1982, p. 32.
[240] Benedikt, Wir fahren nach England, in *Journal 26, Holocaust Survivors '45 Aid Society*, 2002, p. 5.
[241] Klappholz, Gereimte Prosa, Danklied für das UNRRA-Team 182, GFL.
[242] GFP, 1982, p. 30.

[243] Hanus Burger, Die Waisen von Dachau/The Orphans of Dachau, Post-War Newsreels, Imperial War Museum, London, Film and Video Archive, WPN 242-WIF 25.
[244] GFP, 1982, p. 30 f. Author's conversation with Tibor Sands (Munkácsy) in Budapest, March 23, 2012, notes aa-archive. See also Tibor's Remember me? profile, US Holocaust Memorial Museum, http://rememberme.ushmm.org.
[245] Esther Brumberg, staff member of the Museum of Jewish heritage, New York, testified that immediately after the end of the war such photos were taken only at the International D.P. Children's Center Kloster Indersdorf. Notes, aa-archive.
[246] After this assignment, Charles Haacker wanted to adopt Kurt Klappholz. Letter from Pearl Zimmerman to the District Director, UNRRA Eastern Military District, December 13, 1945. UN Archives S-0437-0017-01.
[247] The Author's interviews with Salek Benedikt and Hans Neumann. London , March 2009; Leslie (Lazar) Kleinman, Indersdorf, April 2010. Notes. aa-archive.
[248] Life at K.I., GF notes, GFL.
[249] GFP, 1946, p. 22.
[250] GF film.
[251] GF film.
[252] GF film.
[253] GF film.
[254] GF film.
[255] GFP, 1946, p. 21 f.
[256] Suri Lachmanowicz (born February 10, 1931, today Sarah Kahan), orphaned, was on board the first transport to England. In the camps and in Indersdorf she was friends with Esther Kahan (today Schonefield). Later she married Esther's brother Jack Kahan who was also resident in the International D.P. Children's Center Kloster Indersdorf. Today both are widows living in London. Author's discussion with Sarah Kahan and Esther Schonefield, London, March 2009. Notes, aa-archive. Greta Fischer also detailed Suri Lachmanowicz' search for her father. GFP, 1946, p. 22.
[257] Kent, Courage ..., p. 133.

[258] Author's discussion with Leslie Kleinman at the Indersdorf Reunions in July 2008, July 2009 and April 2010. Notes, aa-archive.

[259] Zoltán Farkas, Report on his experiences during the Holocaust and after liberation, which he was kind enough to give to the Author, aa-archive. Today Zoltán still works as Department Associate for the SLAC of Stanford University, CA. With his brother Erwin he participated in the Indersdorf Reunion in 2008. See also his Remember me? profile, US Holocaust Memorial Museum, http://rememberme.ushmm.org.

[260] Literally 'escape', an illegal Jewish charitable organization. See also Yehuda Bauer, *Flight and Rescue: Brichah*. NY, 1970.

[261] Pavel brought back two girls with him whose brother he had met in Indersdorf. GFP, 1982, p. 31.

[262] GFP, 1982, p. 31.

[263] Jack Terry, email to the Author, May 11, 2010, aa-archive. Jack Terry added that "the only thing I had was knowledge of what one human being can do to another."

[264] Abram Leder, email from his daughter Masha Snaiberg to the Author, May 15, 2010, aa-archive.

[265] The common name among Jews for Palestine before the Israeli state was founded.

[266] Maier Reinstein, email from his daughter Shoshi Friedrich to the Author, May 20, 2010, aa-archive.

[267] UNRRA Subcommittee on Welfare for Europe, Psychological Problems of Displaced Persons, p. 9, IfZ, F1 0.81.

[268] Ibid, p. 24.

[269] "Rückerziehung zum Leben" in Luxemburger Wort, April 23, 1946, p. 5. André Marx Papers, MJH.

[270] Kloeck. "Die Kinder von Indersdorf," *Süddeutsche Zeitung*, December 4, 1945. Interview with Kurt Klappholz, IWM, Reel 23.

[271] Interview with Kurt Klappholz, IWM, Reel 23.

[272] Life at K. I., GF notes, p. 7-8, GFL.

[273] GFP, 1982, p. 12.

[274] Marion E. Hutton. Acting Director, UNRRA Team 182, Report to the UNRRA District Child Welfare Supervisor, District 5, February 14, 1946, UN Archives, S-0436-0039-01.

[275] Recollections on Hell, Holocaust Autobiography by Morris Stein (Moszek Sztajnkeler), April-June 1995. Morris Stein kindly gave his report to the Author. After he had learned a little English, he worked for a time in a meat processing plant. In 1948 he volunteered for the Israeli army. After Israel became a state he earned his living there as a construction worker and finally emigrated to the USA in 1961. He was an employee and grocery store owner until retirement in 1997. Today he lives with his family in North Carolina. Emails to the Author, aa-archive.
[276] GFP, 1982, p. 41.
[277] GF film.
[278] GF film.
[279] GF film.
[280] UNRRA Subcommittee on Welfare for Europe, Psychological Problems of Displaced Persons, p. 13, IfZ, F1.01.81.
[281] Interview with Michael Roth, July 2009, aa-archive.
[282] Kent. Courage ... p. 118. Roman Kniker (Kent), while trying to buy musical instruments for the "Happy Boys Band" on the Czech black market, was jailed for a night. Ibid., p. 131 f. For more about the "Happy Boys Band" see Jack Eisner. *Die Happy Boys. Eine jüdische Band in Deutschland 1945-1949* . Berlin, 2004.
[283] Kent, Courage ..., p. 120.
[284] Bernat Zelikovits drove an American jeep into the fountain in front of Kloster Indersdorf. Later he changed his name to Bernat Zelk and became a taxi driver in Canada. The Author's telephone interview with Zelk's widow Uta Zelk, July 2008. Notes, aa-archive.
[285] Letter from Sister Dolorosa to her Mother Superior, September 20, 1945, Archive H.I.
[286] GF film.
[287] Iwan Kisz (today Irving Klein, USA) gave the Author a copy of this poster in July 2008, aa-archive. Roman Kent told the Author in Jerusalem, 2009, that he had drawn it. Notes, aa-archive.
[288] Discussion with Zoltán and Erwin Farkas, July 2008 in Indersdorf, Notes, aa-archive.

[289] Newspaper article from 1994, David Klappholz's private archive, aa-archive.
[290] Interview with Kurt Klappholz, IWM, Reel 24.
[291] Ibid, IWM, Reel 25.
[292] Ibid.
[293] Letter from Sister Dolorosa to her Mother Superior, September 10, 1945. Archive H.I.
[294] Ibid.
[295] Ibid.
[296] Ibid.
[297] Ibid.
[298] Interview with Kurt Klappholz, IWM, Reel 25; Interview with Salek (Israel) Benedikt and Manfred Heyman (Haymann) March 2009, London, aa-archive; Gilbert "The Boys" p. 273; Kurt Klappholz, Morris (Mojze) Besserman (obituary) in *Journal 9, Holocaust Survivors '45 Aid Society*, 1981.
[299] GFP, 1982, p. 27.
[300] Marion E. Hutton, Acting Director, UNRRA Team 182, Report to UNRRA District Child Welfare Supervisor, UN Archives.
[301] Die UNRRA in der Marienanstalt, p. 2, Archive H.I.
[302] GF film.
[303] Zahava Stessel's mail to the Author, May 1, 2012. aa-archives.
[304] Moshe Ganan's mail to the Author, May 2, 2012. aa-archives.
[305] Marion E. Hutton, Acting Director, UNRRA Team 182, Report to the UNRRA District Child Welfare Supervisor, UN Archives.
[306] GF film..
[307] GFP, 1946, p. 21.
[308] Miriam Warburg who visited the near-by large DP camp Föhrenwald in September 1945, noticed that among grown-up and juvenile survivors "only a quarter of all inmates of the camp work. Three-quarters go idle. Most of them do not want to work. Some say: 'Let the Germans work now. We have worked enough'. Some say: 'Why should I work? It will not bring back what I have lost'. I have heard a sentence repeated by Jews in France and by Jews here, expressed differently according to their

education and their ability of expressing themselves, but I have heard it over and over again: 'I have died long ago. What does it matter, what I do?!'" Warburg, Conditions of Jewish Children, p. 5. IfZ, Fi 01.81.

[309] XX Corps Regional Office, UNRRA, APO 757, October 17, 1945. R.G. Mastrude, Acting Regional Supervisor, H. Zilka, Field Supervisor, Field Supervision Report, DP Children's Center, Kloster Indersdorf, Team 182, October 16, 1945, p. 4.

[310] UNRRA Monthly Team Report, April 30, 1946, André Marx, UN Archives, S-0436-0039-01.

[311] J.E., Die Kinder von Indersdorf, in *Neue Zeitung*, October 25, 1945.

[312] GF film.

[313] GFP, 1946, p. 27.

[314] GF film.

[315] GF film.

[316] GFP, 1982, p. 17.

[317] GFP, 1982, p. 15.

[318] GF film.

[319] UNRRA Monthly Team Report, September 15, 1945, UN Archives.

[320] For instance, a Ukrainian priest came from neighboring Karlsfeld to perform the Sunday mass and give religious instruction. Yugoslavian children attended the Protestant service in Munich. UNRRA Team Report, Team No. 182, April 30, 1946, André Marx, UN Archives.

[321] Angelika Eder, Flüchtige Heimat. Jüdische Displaced Persons in Landsberg am Lech 1945 bis 1950, Munich, 1998, p. 176.

[322] Manfred Haymann was born in 1929, a German Jew, in Stettin. Interview with Manfred Heyman, London, March 2009. Notes, aa-archive.

[323] Ibid.

[324] UNRRA Team Report, Team no. 182, April 30, 1946, André Marx. UN Archives.

[325] In January 1946 the first exclusively Jewish children's home was opened in Strüth near Ansbach. Tobias, *Vorübergehende Heimat*, p. 207 ff.

[326] GFP 1946, III (2) Content of Cultural and Recreational Expression, n.p.
[327] GFP, 1982, p. 16.
[328] GFP, 1982, p. 17.
[329] Lillian D. Robbins, General Description and Background of Children Being Moved to Switzerland for Temporary Care, November 12, 1945, GFN, aa-archive.
[330] GFP 1982, p. 22.
[331] GFP, 1946, III (3) Social relationships, p. 2.
[332] Ibid. Greta Fischer's 1982 text uses the word 'song,' not carols. GFP, 1982, p. 38.
[333] Recommendations, p. 1, UN Archives.
[334] GFP, 1946, p. 21.
[335] Benedikt, "Wir fahren nach England," *Journal 16, Holocaust Survivors '45 Aid Society*, 2002, p. 6.
[336] The Author's phone conversation with Stefanie Watolla (today Wieczorek, Poland) in November 2011, notes aa-archive.
[337] In the American Zone, Jewish and Gentile DPs were at first housed together. President Harry S. Truman sent as government representative Earl G. Harrison (1899-1955) working under the US Commission for Immigration to inspect living conditions in the camps. The inspection team that included members of the AJJDC visited about 30 DP camps in Germany and Austria and presented their report on August 24, 1945. Harrison sharply criticized housing conditions and recommended setting up special camps for Jewish DPs. "Jews as Jews (and not as nationals of the countries where they had been resident) experienced significantly greater persecution than Gentile people of the same or other nationalities." If special recognition were not now accorded to Jews, Harrison reasoned, that meant "closing one's eyes to their earlier, far more barbaric treatment which of itself made them into a special group with greater needs." The report's critique actually led to significant improvement in the camps. Tobias and Schlichting, *Heimat auf Zeit*, p. 21 ff.
[338] In September 1945 efforts were made in the American Zone to group all Jewish children in the DP camp Föhrenwald. Warburg. Conditions of Jewish Children p. 4, IfZ, Fi 01.81. See also

Jim G. Tobias, *Die vergessenen Kinder von Strüth*, TV documentary, Medienwerkstatt Franken, Nuremberg 2001.
[339] GFP, 1982, p. 28.
[340] Erwin Farkas in filmed interview, July 2008, Bettina Witte/Anna Andlauer, *Aus der Hölle ins Leben*, TV documentary, ZDF 2009.
[341] GFP, 1982, p. 36.
[342] ORT, short for Opbschtschestwo Rasprostranenija Truda, was founded in 1880 as a society for artisans in St. Petersburg. Later this developed into the International World ORT Union (Organization for Rehabilitation through Training). The German branch of this Jewish international educational institution was disbanded by the Nazis in 1943. In August 1945 Jacob Oleiski, a Lithuanian Jew, opened in the DP camp Landsberg the first school for technical education in the American Zone. Jacob Oleiski, before the war director of the Lithuanian ORT, was transported from the Kovno Ghetto to Dachau. Immediately following his liberation he took up again his pre-war activities and thereby set the stage for the first ORT school in postwar Germany after the motto "Plan for your future – learn a trade!" Tobias and Schlichting, *Heimat auf Zeit*, p. 80 f.
[343] UNRRA Monthly Team Report, September 15, 1945, p.7 f, UN Archives.
[344] J. E., Die Kinder von Indersdorf, in *Neue Zeitung*, October 25, 1945.
[345] UNRRA Monthly Team Report, March 30, 1946, André Marx, Welfare, Supplementary Sheet, UN Archives.
[346] GFP, 1982, p. 22.
[347] Extract from Monthly Army Inspection Report, Field Supervisor Bakeman, February 21, 1946, UN Archives S-0436-0039-01.
[348] GFP, 1946, p. 29.
[349] Interview Kurt Klappholz, IWM, Reel 25.
[350] Marie Syrkin. The D.P. School qtd in Tobias/Schlichting, Heimat auf Zeit, 56.
[351] Ibid. 16.
[352] UNRRA Monthly Team Report, July 15, 1946, Greta Fischerova, Welfare Supplementary Sheet, UN Archives.

[353] GFP, 1982, p. 22.
[354] Ibid.
[355] A kibbutz is an agricultural collective.
[356] UNRRA Monthly Team Report, April 30, 1946, André Marx, Welfare Supplementary Sheet, UN Archives.
[357] Jacob Oleiski, Schöpferische Arbeit der Sinn des Lebens, [Creative Work Gives Meaning to Life], Speech held to celebrate the opening of the school in the DP camp Landsberg on October 1, 1945, qtd. in Tobias/Schlichting, *Heimat auf Zeit*, p. 81.
[358] UNRRA Monthly Team Report, March 30, 1946, André Marx, Welfare Supplementary Sheet, UN Archives.
[359] UNRRA Subcommittee on Welfare for Europe, Psychological Problems of Displaced Persons, p. 26, IfZ, FI 01.81.
[360] UNRRA Monthly Team Report, March 30, 1946, André Marx, Welfare Supplementary Sheet, UN Archives.
[361] Josef Lichtenstajn's Remember me? profile, US Holocaust Memorial Museum, http://rememberme.ushmm.org.
[362] Recommendations , p. 4, UN Archives.
[363] GFP, 1982, p. 37.
[364] UNRRA Monthly Team Report, March 30, 1946, André Marx, Welfare Supplementary Sheet, UN Archives.
[365] UNRRA Monthly Team Report, April 30, 1946, B. Recreation, p. 4. UN Archives, S-0437-0017-06.
[366] J.E. Die Kinder von Indersdorf in *Neue Zeitung*, October 25, 1945.
[367] GFP, 1982, p. 34.
[368] Miklos Roth remembers a broad selection of skis and sleds for this purpose. Discussion with the Author, July 2008. Indersdorf. Notes, aa-archive.
[369] The bills for these repairs were sent to the local mayor, the Dachau county council or the building authority in Munich. UNRRA Monthly Team Report, September 15, 1945, UN Archives.
[370] Marion E. Hutton, Acting Director, UNRRA Team 182, Report to UNRRA District Child Welfare Supervisor, UN Archives.
[371] Ibid.
[372] GF film.
[373] GFP, 1946, p. 6.

[374] The UNRRA team eventually used cans for this purpose in which powdered milk had been delivered and had Indersdorf artisans fit them out with wooden casings gaily decorated with a blue and white Bavarian lozenge pattern. GF film.
[375] GFP, 1946, p. 30.
[376] GFP, 1982, p. 10.
[377] GF film.
[378] GFP, 1982, p. 10.
[379] Jörg Skriebeleit, *Erinnerungsort Flossenbürg. Akteure, Zäsuren, Geschichtsbilder*, p. 87. Göttingen 2009.
[380] GFP, 1982, p. 3 ff.
[381] Recommendations, p. 4., UN Archives.
[382] GFP, 1982, p. 11.
[383] Marion E. Hutton, Acting Director, UNRRA Team 182, Report to the UNRRA District Child Welfare Supervisor, UN Archives.
[384] Ibid.
[385] Jacobmeyer, *Vom Zwangsarbeiter zum heimatlosen Ausländer*, p. 85.
[386] The children remained in Switzerland for a considerable amount of time to recover; they had not emigrated there. Afterward, most were repatriated to Poland, UNRRA Monthly Team Report, July 15, 1946, UN Archives.
[387] GFP, 1946, p. 8.
[388] Letter from Jean Margaret Henshaw to Pauline Bakeman, Child Welfare Supervisor, Policy of Intake, D.P. Children's Center Kloster Indersdorf, April 10, 1946, Archive of the Dachau Concentration Camp Memorial.
[389] GFP, 1946, p. 8.
[390] In 1944 they had been transported to Germany with their school classes from Hobgart and Bratislava, had learned German and worked in various places. At the end of the war most had been brought to a camp near Bernried. They did not experience May 8, 1945, as liberation day because most had been indoctrinated in Germanization programs and forced to work on farms or in forests. They learned of the war's end only months later. When Helen Steiger took down their personal information, many of them named teachers and others in charge who had accompanied

them. Some of these leaders had already been identified as Nazis and captured. In Indersdorf, the girls and boys showed photos of their relatives and wanted to go home as quickly as possible. D.P. Supplementary Records for Identifying and Tracing Special Categories of Displaced Person, March 9, 1946. Archive of the Dachau Concentration Camp Memorial.

[391] Marion E. Hutton, Acting Director, UNRRA Team 182, Report to the UNRRA District Child Welfare Supervisor, UN Archives.

[392] Ibid.

[393] Screening teams verified the right of DPs in camps to that status.

[394] UNRRA Monthly Team Report, March 30, 1946, UN Archives.

[395] Die UNRRA in der Marienanstalt, p. 5. Archive H.I. In particular, the nuns list women from Estonia, Lithuania, Latvia, Poland, Ukraine, Hungary, Romania and Yugoslavia as having had relations with Americans.

[396] GFP, 1982, p. 35.

[397] GFP, 1946, p. 33.

[398] Thus on November 27, 1945, Mildred G. Wayne of Memphis, Tennessee, contacted the UNRRA after she had seen photos and read an article in her local paper about 202 orphans at Kloster Indersdorf. She wanted to adopt a little girl about five years old. UN Archives, S-0401-0001-01.

[399] GF film.

[400] GFP, 1946, p. 25.

[401] GFP, 1946, p. 33.

[402] Ibid.

[403] Poem by Kurt Klappholz, Salek Benedikt, Hans Neumann and others. October 1945. The poem was kindly given to the Author by Hans Neumann. aa-archive.

[404] Naftali Steinberg later went to Palestine and lives today in Brazil. He came with his friend Abram Leder in 2008 to the Indersdorf Reunion. Notes, aa-archive.

[405] Benedikt, Wir fahren nach England in *Journal 26, Holocaust Survivors '45 Aid Society*, 2002, p. 6 .

[406] GFP, 1982. p. 32. The brothers Zoltán (born December 29, 1928) and Erwin Farkas (born December 28, 1929) were forced to separate from their friend Lazar (Leslie) Kleinmann (born May 29, 1929). But they have kept in touch all their lives and met again during the reunion in Indersdorf, July 2008.
[407] Author's discussion with Alec Ward (Abram Warszaw) in England, March 2009, notes, aa-archive. Email from Morris Stein (Moszek Sztajnkeler), North Carolina, USA, December 2010, aa-archive.
[408] Josef Lichtenstajn's Remember me? profile, US Holocaust Memorial Museum, http://rememberme.ushmm.org.
[409] Author's discussion with Martin Hecht in Indersdorf, July 2011, notes, aa-archive. See also his Remember me? profile, US Holocaust Memorial Museum, http://rememberme.ushmm.org.
[410] Benedikt, Wir fahren nach England in *Journal 26, Holocaust Survivors '45 Aid Society* (2002) p. 6.
[411] Interview with Kurt Klappholz, IWM, Reel 25.
[412] GF film.
[413] Interview with Kurt Klappholz, IWM, Reel 25.
[414] Chaim and Aron Swinik were born in Minsk and survived the Shoah in Siberia with their stepmother; their father died in one of Stalin's camps. In England the two were first taken in by an English foster family and then moved to an orphanage in Oxford. In February 1949, their stepmother, now remarried in Israel, arranged for the two brothers to join her and her husband. Since then they have been living under the name of Rechter in Israel. Emails from Aron Rechter to the Author, January/February 2010, aa-archive.
[415] Die UNRRA in der Marienanstalt, p. 1, Archive H.I.
[416] Ibid.
[417] These Jewish refugees had flown "to the West, escaping from anti-Semitic attacks in their homelands. During the war they had survived in Soviet exile, in the underground or as partisans in the forests. Among them were 25,000 children and young people up to age 18. This group in particular was severely traumatized, had been deprived of an opportunity to develop their sense of social responsibility or ethics, had never been to kindergarten or to

school or had any training in a trade." Tobias and Schlichting, 1982, p. 7.

[418] Peter Lane Taylor, Off the Face of the Earth. The remarkable story of a group of Holocaust survivors who hid in one of the world's largest caves. http://www.aish.com/63053312.html

[419] Sol D. Wexler's video interview, May 29, 1996, Survivors of the Shoah Visual History Foundation, Los Angeles. The tape was kindly given to the Author by Sol D. Wexler.

[420] GFP, 1982, p. 10 (Szlama Wechselblatt, see group photo in chapter "Jewish Child Survivors").

[421] Author's discussion with Miklos (Michael) Roth, Erwin and Zoltán Farkas, Indersdorf, July 2008. Notes, aa-archive.

[422] GFP, 1982, p. 20.

[423] Teachers, youth leaders.

[424] Author's interview with Jewish survivor Karl Rom who worked with the Bricha from mid-1945 to mid-1948. Weichs, October 2010. Notes, aa-archive.

[425] Youth Aliyah (meaning to rise up, immigrate to Israel) was founded in 1933 to save Jewish youths from Nazi Germany. After the war it brought many young Jewish Holocaust survivors and refugees to Palestine.

[426] Itzchak Gilboa's mail to the Author, April 29, 2012. aa-archive.

[427] Hebrew for "Revolution."

[428] On May 13, 1946, the group called a one-day hunger and labor strike. Discussion with the director led to fulfillment of some of their demands. The administration, however, wanted the group to integrate itself into the Children's Center. UNRRA Team Monthly Report, May 25, 1946, André Marx, UN Archives, S-0436.0039.01.

[429] Zahava Szász Stessel, *Snow Flowers. Hungarian Women in an Airplane Factory, Markkleeberg, Germany*, Madison, NJ, 2009, p. 296.

[430] GFP, 1982, p. 41.

[431] Die UNRRA in der Marienanstalt, 1982, p. 41 f.

[432] Moshe Ganan's mail to the Author, May 2, 2012. aa-archive.

[433] Ibid.

[434] Today Katalin Száz is Zahava Stessel and lives in New York City; her younger sister Erzsébet is Hava Ginsburg and lives in Israel.
[435] Moshe Ganan's mail to the Author, May 14, 2012, aa-archives.
[436] D.P. Children's Center UNRRA Team 182, Kloster Indersdorf, May 13, 1946. Report from Jean Margaret Henshaw and Cornelia Heise, Zone Child Welfare Office, aa-archive.
[437] The UNRRA existed until July 1, 1947, when the IRO (International Refugee Organization) took over responsibility for DPs.
[438] Meeting of the Board of Liberated Jews in Bavaria, October 14, 1945, Minutes No. 13, qtd. in Tobias/Schlichting, *Heimat auf Zeit*, p. 39 f.
[439] GFP, 1982, p. 32.
[440] GFP, 1982, p. 34.
[441] Telephone interview with Genia Edlermann (Jean Sugar) October 21, 2010. aa-archive. Since this postwar period Nehemia Edlermann has lived in Israel and his sister Genia in Canada.
[442] GFP, 1982, p. 30.
[443] Interviews with Zoltán and Erwin Farkas and Michael Roth in July 2008 in Indersdorf; interview with Steve Israeler in July 2010 in Indersdorf. Notes, aa-archive.
[444] GFP, 1982, p. 24.
[445] GFP, 1946, II. (4) Army Mascots. n.p.
[446] Ibid.
[447] Sergeant Jack Dunwoodie from Buffalo, NY, had agreed to adopt him and take him home. Children at D.P. Children's Center Kloster Indersdorf who wish to apply for visas for the United States of America. March 13, 1946, Archive of the Dachau Concentration Camp Memorial.
[448] GFP, 1946, p. 16 f. Michael Kolesnik was born in 1930 in Vinnitsa, Ukraine. His parents soon died. In 1942 he was deported to Germany. After liberation he was cared for at Kloster Indersdorf and moved with the International D.P. Chhildren's Center to Prien on Chiemsee. From there he was repatriated at the end of 1946 to the Soviet Union. International Children's Center on Chiemsee, UNRRA Team Report 188, List of Ukrainian and

Russian Children, October 1, 1946, UN Archives, S-0437-0017-01.

[449] GFP, 1946, p. 32.

[450] GFP, 1982, p. 22.

[451] GFP, 1946, p. 32.

[452] GFP, 1946, p. 31.

[453] Ibid.

[454] UNRRA Monthly Team Report, April 30, 1946, Jean Margaret Henshaw, UN Archives, S-0436-0039-01.

[455] Children from Germany who arrived on S.S. Champollion on April 25, 1946, Central Zionist Archives, Jerusalem (CZA), S 756/4857.

[456] Abram Leder. Memories from my Home in Poland and from the Holocaust. Report, aa-archive. Even though the British authorities in Palestine made it difficult for Jewish survivors to immigrate to the Mandate, from time to time legal options for individuals arose. The first legal transport for Palestine left Indersdorf on April 9, 1946. Jewish Agency for Palestine, Letter from Dr. Chaim Hoffmann to J. Taylor, Chief Field Supervisor Child Welfare Department, April 6, 1946, UN Archives, S-0434-0017-05.

[457] The Jewish Agency for Palestine was the official representative to the British Mandate for Jews living in Palestine.

[458] An agricultural cooperative in Israel.

[459] Abram Leder. Memories, aa-archive.

[460] Altogether, 732 young Jewish survivors found refuge in Great Britain. Even today they call themselves "The Boys" and are members of the *Survivors '45 Aid Society*. Author's discussion with Salek (Israel) Benedikt, Alec Ward (Abram Warszaw), Martin Hecht, Ben Helfgott, Manfred Heyman (Haymann) and others, London, March 2009. Notes, aa-archive.

[461] Herb Krosney, *The Boys. Triumph over Adversity*, DVD, Krosney Productions 2006. Comments from some of the "Boys" regarding their shared time in English hostels. They belive this had a benficial effect on how they later managed their lives.

[462] Die UNRRA in der Marienanstalt, p. 5, Archive H.I.

[463] Margaret Wiesender, Edna M. Davis, Report: Repatriation to Poland of Unaccompanied Children from Children's Centers at

Wartenberg, Deggendorf and Kloster Indersdorf, June 21, 1946, p. 1. Displaced Persons – Children – Repatriation and Resettlement 8/10/1945 – 17/12/1945, UN Archives, S-0437-0017-06.

[464] Only two Polish youths refused to go back to Poland. UNRRA Monthly Team Report. July 15, 1946, UN Archives.

[465] Robbins, "Refugees – who cares?" GFP, USHMM, RG-19.034*04.

[466] Jean Margaret Henshaw, the second director of the Children's Center, claimed that lack of empathy on the part of the liaison officers and lack of understanding for the needs of teens were responsible. UNRRA Monthly Team Report, July 15, 1946, UN Archives.

[467] GFP, 1946, II. (5) Family Relations – Voluntary Separation, n.p.

[468] Ruth S. Feder, UNRRA PI Correspondent in UNRRA Team News, Vol. 2, No. 1, DP Operations, Germany, January 8, 1947, GFL, p. 7.

[469] GFP, 1946, p. 31.

[470] Walter Beringer, Die UNRRA im Kloster Indersdorf, in *Jahresbericht der Realschule Vinzenz von Paul*, Indersdorf 1994/95. The children's center in Prien appears in AJJDC statistics for the first time on July 31, 1946. Tobias/Schlichting. *Heimat auf Zeit*. 118.

[471] See footnote 148.

[472] GFP, 1982, p. 40. See also the chapter Struggling to Restore Health.

[473] GF film.

[474] International Children Center at Prien, Report by Tessy Y. Sokol, Medical Social Consultant, p. 3 f., Germany, Displaced Persons Camps A-Z, 1945-1948. AJIDC, Givat Joint Archives, Jerusalem, NY 45/54, #324.

[475] Even the owners of the Strandhotel, the Merklstetters, were forbidden to set foot in the building during that time. Despite the place being off limits, Hannemie Johannes, daughter of the owners, nonetheless became friends with one of the boys with whom she kept in touch all her life. In 2008 she supported a reunion of Jewish survivors in their former hotel. Discussion with the Author and Hannemie Johannes in April 2008. Notes, aa-archive.

[476] International Children Center at Prien, Report by Tessy Y. Sokol, Medical Social Consultant, p. 3 f., AJJDC, Givat Joint Archives, Jerusalem.

[477] Ibid. In this document, Hotel Kampenwand is mistakenly called Kempenwald.

[478] "These foreign personnel were the reason why it took so long before transferring the babies and toddlers. Miss Fischerova used to say, 'In Indersdorf I have the Sisters who are completely devoted to the children's care so that I can leave the house at any time while in Gstadt I have no one whom I can absolutely trust'." Die UNRRA in der Marienanstalt, p. 6, Archive H.I.

[479] Ibid. p. 5.

[480] Ibid.

[481] Report by Etta Deutsch, September/October 1946, Tobias/Schlichting, Heimat auf Zeit, p. 118 f.

[482] International Children's Center at Prien, Report by Tessy Y. Sokol, Medical Social Consultant, p. 8 AJJDC, Givat Joint Archives, Jerusalem.

[483] Die UNRRA in der Marienanstalt, p. 7, Archive H.I.

[484] International Children's Center at Prien, Report by Tessy Y. Sokol, Medical Social Consultant, p. 6, AJJDC, Givat Joint Archives, Jerusalem.

[485] Ibid. p. 7.

[486] Tobias/Schlichting, *Heimat auf Zeit*, p. 40 f.

[487] Robbins, "Refugees – who cares?" GFP, USHMM, RG-19.034*04.

[488] Ibid.

[489] GF film.

[490] GF film.

[491] GF film.

[492] GFP, 1982, p. 46.

[493] GFP, 1982, p. 46.

[494] In the end Canada took 1,123 young orphaned Holocaust survivors from DP camps in Germany. The first group arrived in Halifax on September 15, 1947. Fraidie Martz, *Open Your Hearts. The Story of the Jewish War Orphans in Canada.* Montreal 1996, p. 17 ff.

[495] GF film.

[496] Moshe Ganan's mail to the Author, April 28, 2012. aa-archive.
[497] Ibid.
[498] UNRRA Team 182 in Indersdorf would later become Team 1066 and Team 1067. The center began to serve "Jewish Infiltree unaccompanied children" exclusively, as the young refugees from Central and Eastern Europe were called who at the end of the war had not been staying in territories that had belonged to the German Reich. Children's Centers, G.K. Richman, Assistant Director Relief Services Division to UNRRA Central Headquarters, Arolsen, August 15, 1946, UN Archives, S-0425-0054-05.
[499] UNRRA Monthly Team Report, September 15, 1946, Karl H.V. Berthold, UN Archives, S-0436-0039-01.
[500] Dror – literally "freedom" – a left-Zionist youth organization.
[501] Report by Shulamit Katz, Hashomer Hatzair Archives, Kibbutz Givat Haviva (Israel), Document No. (66)14.13.2. Manuscript of the unpublished partial translation by Zwi Katz, aa-archive.
[502] Ibid.
[503] Ibid.
[504] Tobias/Schlichting, *Heimat auf Zeit*, p. 116.
[505] Author's discussion with Ester Katz, April 2009, Indersdorf, and Henia Marcus, January 2009, Jerusalem. Notes, aa-archive.
[506] UNRRA Monthly Area Team Report, Team 1067, November 15, 1946, UN Archives, S-0436-0012-05.
[507] Ibid.
[508] Ibid.
[509] Moshe Ganan's mail to the Author, April 28, 2012. aa-archive.
[510] Report by Shulamit Katz, Hashomer Hatzair Archives, Kibbutz Givat Haviva (Israel).
[511] Tobias/Schlichting, *Heimat auf Zeit*, p. 77, p. 117.
[512] Fred Zinnemann, *The Search* (German: *Die Gezeichneten*), USA/Switzerland 1948.
[513] Report by Shulamit Katz, Hashomer Hatzair Archives, Kibbutz Givat Haviva (Israel).

[514] The first Romanian groups reached Vienna in April 1947. Following a transit lay-over in Austria, the children traveled on to Germany. Altogether in 1947 alone, 19,000 Jews left Romania. Bauer, *Flight and Rescue*, p. 298.

[515] Letter from David Umanski, October 19, 1947, qtd. in Tobias/Schlichting. *Heimat auf Zeit*, p. 117.

[516] Tobias/Schlichting, *Heimat auf Zeit*, p. 117.

[517] Report by Shulamit Katz, Hashomer Hatzair Archives, Kibbutz Givat Haviva (Israel).

[518] Tobias/Schlichting, *Heimat auf Zeit*, p. 129.

[519] UNRRA Subcommittee on Welfare for Europe, Psychological Problems of Displaced Persons, p. 25, IfZ, FI. 0I.8I.

[520] Ibid.

[521] "Americans" here means the UNRRA Team 182 in Kloster Indersdorf.

[522] Kloeck, Die Kinder von Indersdorf, in *Süddeutsche Zeitung*, December 4, 1945.

[523] Ibid.

[524] Mathilde Oftedal, speech during a US Senate committee meeting in Washington, July 1947.

[525] GFP, 1946, III (9) Reaction to Stabilized Living, n.p.

[526] GFP, 1982, p. 4.

[527] GFP, 1982, Ibid.p. 446.

[528] The following biographical information was gleaned from discussions between the Author and the former residents of Kloster Indersdorf. Notes, aa-archive. In the documentary *Children of the Storm*, Jack Kuper explores the stories of the young survivors in Canada. Kuper Productions, Canada 2001. In the documentary *The Boys. Triumph over Adversity*. Herb Krosney focuses on the lives of the Jewish orphans who settled in England. Krosney productions 2006.

[529] "A rage to know" or "a rage to understand." Discussion with the Author during the reunion in Indersdorf, July 2011, aa-archives.

[530] It is not unlikely that most of those repatriated to the Soviet Union or Poland would have had a much harder time so that their "rediscovery" might have led to different conclusions.

[531] Fraidie Martz, "How Child Survivors Came To Canada" Newspaper article, aa-archives. 1990

[532] Kent, *Courage was my only option*, p. 358.

[533] Roman Kent and his brother Leon started out as department store assistants. Leon became a surgeon and later died at 46 of a tumor. Roman Kent became a successful businessman. Today he is the treasurer of the Jewish Claims Conference, Chairman of the "American Gathering of Jewish Holocaust Survivors," and President of the International Auschwitz Committee. Kent, *Courage ...*, p. 154 ff.

[534] Kurt Klappholz was at the London School of Economics at the same time as Mick Jagger and was his teacher. Klappholz is said to have advised Jagger to devote himself to music rather than to economics which in turn led to his launch of the "Rolling Stones." Interview with Salek Benedikt, London, March 2009. Notes, aa-archive.

[535] Patricia De Landtsheer, *Bewaar Altijd Een Stukje Brood*. Antwerpen, 2001.

[536] Moshe Ganan's mail to the Author, May 16, 2012. aa-archive.

[537] Jadwiga Schulikowska's Remember me? profile, US Holocaust Memorial Museum, http://rememberme.ushmm.org.

[538] Author's conversation with Tibor Sands on March 23, 2012 in Budapest. At the beginning of the 1960s Tibor Sands also took photos for Lillian D. Robbins, when the former director of the Indersdorf Children's Center was executive director at Lenox Hill Neighbourhood Association in New York.

[539] Peter Lane Taylor, Christos Nicola, The Secret of Priest's Grotto. A Holocaust Survival Story, Minneapolis, 2007.

[540] Filmed interview with Zoltán Farkas, Shoah Foundation, California. Quoted with permission of Zoltán Farkas.

[541] Interview with Zoltán Farkas, July 2008, notes aa-archive. "Gloomy Sunday" is a song composed by Hungarian pianist and composer Rezso Serres and published in 1933.

[542] Eugenius Kamer's Remember me? profile, US Holocaust Memorial Museum, http://rememberme.ushmm.org

[543] GFP, 1982, p. 46.

[544] GF film.

[545] GF film.
[546] Remembering Greta, Canada 1988; Letter from Ruth Lemco to Micha Plaschkes on Greta Fischer's death, GFL.
[547] Until 1939, Stanislawów was Polish. Today the place is called Ivano-Frankivsk and belongs to the Ukraine.
[548] Remembering Greta, GFL.
[549] It was only after the war that Greta Fischer learned of her parents' death. GF film and the Author's interview with Greta Fischer's nephew Micha Plaschkes, Israel, January 2010. Notes, aa-archive.
[550] Greta Fischer's Certificate of Registration no. 733081, Aliens Order, London 1939-1945, GFL.
[551] See Greta Fischer, From Awareness – to Action, presented at the Canadian Gathering of Jewish Holocaust Survivors and their Children, Ottawa 1985, GFL.
[552] GF, Supplementary Material, p. 1. GFL.
[553] GF film.
[554] Ibid.
[555] In this document her forty co-workers thank "our dear director and guardian" "Greta Fischerova." GFL. Greta Fischer never wanted to be called "Fischerova" and officially deleted the Czech suffix at the end of the 1940s in Canada. Passports, GFL.
[556] The UNRRA existed until July 1, 1947. After that the IRO (International Refugee Organization) took over care for DPs. Greta Fischer was offered a contract that would have extended the work she had been doing for the UNRRA, but she declined.
[557] GF, Supplementary material, p.1, GFL.
[558] From 1953 to 1955, Greta Fischer studied education part-time at McGill University in Montreal. Greta Fischer's resume "Personal History," p. 1, GFL.
[559] Greta Fischer, Supplementary Material, p. 2, GFL.
[560] "Working villages," GF resume, "Personal History," p. 3, GFL.
[561] Discussion of the Author with Rita Abramov, Estelle Rubinstein, Dina Wardi, Ronnie Gertel, Prof. Jona Rosenfeld and Dr. Varda Soskone, Jersusalem, January 2010. Notes, aa-archive.
[562] GFP, 1982.
[563] Greta Fischer, Supplementary Material, p. 1, GFL.

[564] Discussion of the Author and Dina Wardi, Lilo Plaschkes and Esther Halevi, Israel, January 2009 and January 2010. Notes, aa-archive.

[565] In Kloster Indersdorf Greta Fischer learned that Kurt Klappholz had been in a concentration camp together with Greta's Czech boyfriend. Kurt told her that her friend had shared his bread with Kurt but had not survived. Greta Fischer: "But this boy did survive and I feel very warm-hearted toward him." GF film.

[566] Author's interview with Jack and Maureen Hecht, London, February 2009. Notes, aa-archive.

[567] Remembering Greta, Ruth Lemco to Micha Plaschkes, GFL.

[568] Interview with Rita Abramov, Director of the social work department, Hadassah Hospital, Jerusalem, January 20, 2010. Notes, aa-archive.

[569] Ibid.

[570] Conference contributions to Greta Fischer's 100th jubilee on January 19, 2010, at Hadassah Hospital and contributions of co-workers, relatives and friends on the occasion of her 99th birthday in the Abramov house, Jerusalem. Notes aa-archive.

[571] Fraidie Martz, email to the Author March 30, 2011, aa-archives.

[572] Daniela Gorgs, „Im Geist der Liebe" in *Süddeutsche Zeitung*, Dachau regional supplement, July 2, 2010.

Made in the USA
Charleston, SC
09 December 2016